SMART MONEY

4 Key Finance Strategies To Set Yourself Up For The Future

Tracey contacted me to say that she had organised a pricing request on my current home loan and had saved me $4,000 a year in my repayments. I have never had a broker do this before off their own back and this is why I refer all my family and friends to Tracey at FinanceCorp.

Sandra & Will Walquist

I can't thank FINANCE CORP enough. I recently got rejected from my own bank and was referred to these guys! Tracey Franco and the FinanceCorp team, went above and beyond and got me a loan! Probably one of the most hardest of people to help (due to bad credit score) but they did it through hard work and dedication. Unbelievable, I'm so happy I got them to be my brokers! Thank you so much ANGELA, TRACEY AND BIANCA. I can't recommend them highly enough! Absolutely the best! Thank you thank you thank you!!!

Michelle Fearon

Tracey and her team at Finance Corp deliver a fantastic, professional service. I have no hesitation in recommending them to my clients.

Tini Mincher

Finance corp is amazing! Super friendly and helpful staff that have your best interests at heart. Highly recommend

Melissa Spadaro

I would highly recommend FinanceCorp Make them your first port of call. They were absolutely fantastic, very professional, friendly and super efficient. I would especially like to give a big Thank you to Tracey & Tiarne, they made what was a difficult time so much easier. They were on the ball, no question was too difficult, they touched base constantly and responded to phone calls very quickly. If you're looking for first class service look no further. Many Thanks.

Nilla Spagnolo

SMART MONEY

4 Key Finance Strategies To Set Yourself Up For The Future

FinanceCorp
Finance Made Easy

Australian Credit Licence 395037

First published 2017 by FinanceCorp

www.financecorp.com.au

Copyright © FinanceCorp and Tracey Franco 2017.

The moral rights of the author have been asserted.

National Library of Australia Cataloguing-in-Publication Entry:

Creator: Franco, Tracey, author.

Title: Smart money : 4 key finance strategies to set yourself
             up for the future / Tracey Franco.

ISBN: 9780648008200 (paperback)
             9780648008217 (ebook)

Subjects: Finance, Personal.
             Budgets, Personal.
             Financial security.
             Property--Economic aspects.
             Success.

Printed in Australia.

Disclaimer

The material in this publication is of the nature of general comment only, and does not represent professional or financial advice. It is not intended to provide specific guidance for particular circumstances and it should not be relied on as the basis for any decision to take action or not take action on any matter which it covers. Readers should obtain professional advice where appropriate, before making any such decision. To the maximum extent permitted by law, the author and publisher disclaim all responsibility and liability to any person, arising directly or indirectly from any person taking or not taking action based upon the information in this publication. Names used in examples and case studies have been changed for privacy reasons.

Want to get smarter with your money and mortgage?

Most people struggle to manage their money properly. Even with regular salaries coming in, they spend too much and end up further and further in debt - and the money worries and stress always follows.

Most people don't know how to correctly setup and manage their mortgage. All too often we hear that "a loan is just a loan, they are all the same", which is false. All loans are not equal and if you don't know what to do you could be set up the wrong way, you could be paying too much, and you could be restricting your options for the future.

But it doesn't have to be that way. You don't have to struggle with your money and you don't have to navigate the minefield of mortgages alone.

This book will start you on the right path towards getting smarter with your money, your mortgage and your financial future.

It's also important that you get expert advice from a professional who understands the finance and mortgage market inside and out. It's simply too difficult and there's too much to try and do it all yourself.

You should speak with a FinanceCorp finance professional today, and get an expert on your side - to ensure you're set up correctly, not paying too much, and are thinking about your financial future.

And the best part is, I will do everything for you!

Start a conversation with me today - I will help you get smarter with your money, mortgage and financial future.

☎ Call me on: **0417 395 949** OR

✉ Send an email to: **traceym@financecorp.com.au**

Tracey Franco
DIRECTOR / MENTOR

"Everything that happens always happens for a reason"

CONTENTS

About the author

With over 18 years of mortgage broking experience under her belt, Tracey Franco took on a typically male-dominated industry - and wiped the floor clean.

She is the owner of the wildly successful FinanceCorp, a leading financial services provider that was nominated for **Business of the Year**, three years in a row! (2014, 2015 & 2016) and #1 brokerage /Business of the Year 2022.

FinanceCorp lives by the motto Finance Made Easy and they have settled in excess of $396 million dollars in loans, helping thousands of clients have a simple and stress-free experience that exceeds all expectations.

Driven by the love for her family and a sense of duty to give back to the community, Tracey and FinanceCorp sponsors many charities, including *Second Harvest* (helping feed under-privileged people throughout the Perth Metro area) as well as the *Intensive Care Foundation* (providing funding for emergency care centres throughout Australia.)

Tracey is an inspirational woman who makes a real difference to thousands of people's financial lives, every day.

Acknowledgements

To Rebecca Little, Amy Western, Dale Robinson, Michelle Ahola, Krys Tully and Eric Franco - thank you for your help with this book; I couldn't have done it without you.

To my mum, for always being there for me no matter what and for always believing in everything I do.

To James Veigli and the Published Author Direct team - thank you for your help in bringing this book to life.

To the FinanceCorp team - on reflection on the things I am most grateful for, I am grateful that I have a talented group of people to work alongside. Thank you for the work you have done for FinanceCorp over the years. You have helped us provide award winning services to all of our clients.

To YOU, our existing and new clients - thank you for trusting me and my team with your financial lives. We are honoured to have the opportunity to work with you and the relationships we have forged and your financial success will always be our first priority. We are here to serve you.

My story

I started my life out very shy and dependent. My sister spoke for me until I was over 3 years old. No one would believe me if I told them that now! I started to play basketball at 6 and was the smallest on the team. Nothing has changed in this regard! To make up for my lack of height, I was the most enthusiastic and competitive team player. Back then we had to play with boys and girls, so this helped me become strong and not allow people to push me around. It also built my confidence.

At 13 I was told that there was no room in the basketball world for small people, and my attitude was well we will see about that! I played basketball 7 days a week and started playing A-grade ladies basketball at 13, and I thrived on it. I was accepted into the basketball scholarship at Willetton High School and played junior State League. This took my parents and family all over the metro area, being my support and a great cheer squad. I won best and fairest trophies for my club and for the stadium multiple times throughout my basketball life.

As a child, I had a love of money; however, we didn't have a lot, as my parents divorced at an early age; so things were rather tight on that front. My mum remarried and we became a blended family, which was not popular in those days. So life was different but fun, as I had a very supportive family and friends, and I had my basketball which was my passion!

I love to be part of a team and work together to achieve a common goal. I always believed that if you came second you were last. I still believe this. I disliked school and I decided in year 11 3/4 that I wasn't going back. Mum said that if I got a job in a child care centre then I could leave. This was to be my career path once I had graduated. I applied for as many jobs I could and after the first interview I nailed it. So off I started on my first adventure in the real world.

I always wanted to make lots of money but wasn't sure what I was going to do to make it. I knew that if I found something that I loved to do and worked hard then the money would come.

I started in finance when I was 18, in a different sector to what I am in now. This was called factoring finance and my boss was a tyrant. However, she taught me a lot about business and how not to treat staff if you want to get the best out of them.

My main goals in life were to have a good job, get married, have a child and pay my house off by the time I was 30; I was a little off in this calculation - I achieved all of these by the time I was 32. I purchased my first investment at 21 and had to save hard to achieve it. When I set myself goals, I make sure I achieve them even if it takes longer than expected.

One of my work goals was that I wanted to work for Coca Cola as a sales rep, so when I was 23 I applied and got the job. I thoroughly enjoyed working for this company. A lot of my sales training came from Coca Cola and I believe that this was the foundation of my great sales career.

After Coca Cola, I was poached back to the finance industry and worked for a few years as a Finance and Insurance Manager for Volvo / Suzuki. Although I enjoyed this job, I decided it would be far more exciting to help people purchase their dream homes instead of cars.

In January 2005, I was lucky enough to start with FinanceCorp and after 12 months I was offered the opportunity to have my own franchise. I jumped at this. I have always enjoyed a challenge and hate saying no to opportunities, so I took the plunge!

By 2008 I had 2 FinanceCorp franchises and then in 2009 I was offered the opportunity to purchase the company. At the time FinanceCorp had 5 offices including mine. I closed the other 4 offices and continued to build up the FinanceCorp business. At this stage I only had the 1 office and around 18 staff.

With the help of my supportive husband we built the company and Recruited more brokers. In 2016, we opened our second office which was in Kelmscott and then we went on, in the same year, to open an office in Melbourne.

We currently have 28 Mortgage brokers and 8 support staff and we are growing fast! We have now included more interstate Mortgage brokers.

I believe that the FinanceCorp team are like my second family and I always try to encourage my staff, as I know they can achieve their goals if they set their mind to it. I am a team player who always tries to see the best in people. Of course, I have made some errors in judgement over the years; however, I don't consider these mistakes. They were opportunities to learn from and perform better next time. I try to live by the motto that it is not the mistake that counts but the time you take to recover.

I have employed staff that have been detrimental to my business. Over the years I have learnt to trust my own judgement. If I think something is not quite right, then I act on my gut feeling. I make my own choices in life and try not to let other people influence my decisions. I make a decision and move forward. I also enjoy seeing my clients' deals get approved, and I want it to be a stress-free process for them. But it is not just about the clients, either. I want the people we work with to be happy with our services and to continue using us because we do a good job.

My main motivation is my family; my daughter and my husband. Making sure they have a good life and have the opportunity to get everything they want in life. I also want to see my staff succeed. It is not just about me. It is about everyone I surround myself with being happy and successful. I guess that is what gets me out of bed in the morning, seeing myself, my family and staff succeeding in life and having all the things they wish for. Because you can have everything you wish for if you work hard.

I have never been to university and I want to get through to young people that it doesn't matter if you have a piece of paper telling you how qualified you are. That won't determine your success. As Sir Richard Branson says, "If you have fun then the money will come." Today life is great because there is structure to everything. I know where I am heading and have learned what not to do. I now have the freedom to do whatever I want.

Introduction

Who is this book for?

This book is for people who are unsure about the process of purchasing a home, people such as first home buyers, people seeking options on affordability to see what they can borrow based on their income, and people looking to buy an investment property. Or you may just be looking for a better interest rate on your home loan.

Many people really don't know much about buying a property and want to know more about mortgages, banks, and what you can and can't do. You may want to extend your business or find out how to reduce financial stress and feel like you are more in control. You may be looking for ways to improve your current financial situation and your security in the future.

There is more to a mortgage than just interest rates and having a deposit. If you go straight to a bank instead of a mortgage broker, they are not necessarily going to have your best interests in mind. Plus, they only have their own products to offer you. FinanceCorp, on the other hand, deals with a range of banks and a range of products offered by multiple lenders.

Once you have spoken to one of our Finance Managers at FinanceCorp, we are going to hold your hand every step of the way and make sure that the process is stress-free for you. Our Finance Managers are motivated to get the best results for their clients every time, just as if they were dealing with a close family member or doing their own loan.

Each bank has a different lending policy. Despite offering an amazing interest rate, that bank's policy might not suit your particular requirements and situation, and you might be better off with another lender; you are not going to know that because you don't know the details of their lending policies. You could also find yourself in a credit trap, and end up borrowing too much money. Yes, the bank will offer you the maximum you can afford, but that may be more than you are comfortable borrowing. That is great for the bank, but it is not great for you, and not good for your credit score, either.

Key Point

It comes down to structure, and this makes a difference. There are a lot of things you can do initially to control your financial future, but there is also some bad advice out there, even in the banks. Better to deal with a team of people that you trust, who are unbiased, and who will give you professional information.

Often clients will go to the bank and speak to a staff member who doesn't actually have any lending experience. The staff member tells them they should be able to borrow a certain amount of money without taking all the necessary details. Based on this information, the client puts in an offer on a house. When they go back to the bank to get their approval, they are told that they don't fit the policy. They have been given the wrong information to begin with.

If you go to a mortgage broker first, we are obliged to take all your information and do the research for you prior to telling you that you can borrow money. We also have a duty of care; we have to make sure that we are putting you into the right product and not leading you up the garden path.

A lot of people, faced with the huge decision of buying a house or an investment property, just decide to do it on a whim or without sufficient information. They just talk to a bank staff member, because they are not aware of the options available to them. They have a loyalty to their bank.

Clients think that they need to be loyal to their bank, but banks are big businesses trying to keep their stakeholders happy. They are not going to change any of their policies to help you get into a loan just because you have been banking with them for 20 years. You may have to go to another bank that you've never banked with, who is happy to assist you with a loan.

A mortgage broker is going to know the majority of the banks' policies. If you don't use a broker, you might go to Bank A, not fit the policy, go to Bank B, and not fit the policy. At Bank C, you might fit the policy, but because you have already been to Bank A and Bank B, Bank C won't give you the loan because you have too many enquiries on your credit report, and therefore don't meet the required credit score. With a broker, we will know straight away that Bank C is the one you are likely to have success with because you don't fit the policies of Bank A and Bank B.

Key Point

When you go to your bank and get knocked back, that actually goes on your credit score, and that can be to your detriment the next time you go to borrow.

There are a lot of variables that you need to consider when looking to borrow money and I hope this book will help you do that.

What is this book about?

The information in this book will hopefully enlighten you and open your eyes to opportunities that you might not know are available to you. It will also help you get on top of your finances and make sure that you are actually in the positive and not the red. If you are a first home buyer, we will chat to you about your first home. We can also talk about expanding into your second home, if that is what you want to do. We can show you how to make your money work for you as well, by paying your mortgage off sooner, or providing information on what you should be doing that most people just don't know about.

This book is also tailored towards people who own their own business. If you want to expand your business, we can advise you about what you need to do when it comes to your finances, and prevent you from getting into trouble with that as well. Securing your future and planning for 'what if' is important. You should always have a backup plan for your business, or even your personal situation. There are always a lot of 'what ifs' if something bad does happen. We can test your readiness to start investing. We can put you in contact with the right people so you can get the right information first up.

> People live beyond their means, and they do that because they don't know what they should be doing. They don't manage their money on an ongoing basis, and their culture of spending is to spend it before they have even got it. They haven't been taught the value of looking after their money.

We want you to use this book to educate yourself so that you don't do that, and help you develop different life attitudes about money and how you use your credit cards.

Who should read this book?

This book is for anyone who wants to understand how their mortgage actually works, and also includes a little bit about how the investment market works. There is a section for first home buyers and the small to medium investor. If you're someone who has a franchise and looking to grow your business, this book is a great read for you as well, to make sure that your lending structure works for you, because with business, everybody's structure is different. Really this book is for anyone who wants to get ahead in life, get some tips and buy some property, commercial or residential.

Our client base is generally the white collar and blue collar worker; most of them are first home buyers and small investors. They are the people who will get the most out of this book, so we have tailored it towards what we feel will benefit them.

You don't necessarily have to do a lot of fancy things to get ahead financially. A lot of books out there about finance, superannuation and investment strategies are really advanced and beyond the average person. This book will be easy to read, one that mum and dad investors will actually read and understand and get something from.

Benefits of reading this book

This book will help you to understand how to get the best finance for your situation. I won't sugar coat anything – it will be straight to the point of what you can actually do. You will also learn how to avoid bad debt. If I can stop someone getting into financial hardship, then that's awesome. Reading this book will give you the confidence to take control of your financial future so you are actually protected moving forward. You need to develop a long-term strategy to get from A to B. If your strategy is to buy your first house and then to buy an investment property in the next few years, you need to know how to get there.

Those are the benefits you are going to get from reading this book – how to achieve greater freedom, security and flexibility for your future. Most people's goal in life is to be financially free, but unfortunately not everyone achieves that.

I am writing this book with the hope of educating people, because at FinanceCorp, we actually care about our clients. We are going to be around long term, not short term, so we want to build relationships with people and see them succeed. That is what we are about.

Tips for reading this book

This book is written in an easy-to-understand way. When reading, I hope you feel like I am having a personal conversation with you one-on-one. Throughout the book you will see special call-out sections, designed to show you the most important take-away points as you go along.

Here's how they work:

Key Point

This icon and style of the call-out box represents the **Key Point** you need to know, so pay close attention to what you see in these boxes. This could be a big mistake to avoid, smart strategy to use, or important tip to help you.

Case Study

Boxes that look like this include Case Studies or Examples you can learn from. Often an idea or topic is best explained by working it through and seeing how the numbers look. It's also a great way of showing you how a strategy or topic works in real life.

This icon and call-out is used to highlight important Quotes from the book, as well as sharing with you quotes and wisdom from other famous people.

Valuable Resource

When you see this icon and call-out, it's because I have a **Valuable Resource** to share with you. This could be a website to view, document, template or calculator to download; or contact information for you to get professional assistance. Not everything can fit inside this book – so keep an eye out for these extra resources to help.

Before we begin

So we are clear right from the start, this book is a general educational guide only, and is definitely not a substitute for specific financial advice. If anyone ever gives you advice without first understanding your full situation and goals, my advice is simple: run!

Introduction

Before taking any action on anything you learn in this book, or anywhere else for that matter, please seek professional advice from a licensed expert. That means getting your tax advice from an accountant, financial advice from a financial planner, credit and lending advice from a licensed finance broker, property advice from a real estate agent (or buyer's agent), and legal advice from a solicitor.

Accept no less than credible, authorised and specific expert advice at all times, and always make sure you are well informed before making any decisions.

Please retain this book in a convenient location so that you may refer to it in the future, and feel free to ask for additional copies as a means to introducing those you care about and feel will benefit from this information.

I hope you enjoy this book and learn important information to help you on your property journey.

Here's to your future!

Tracey Maree Franco

CHAPTER 1

Money matters

Attitudes toward money

In this chapter we are going to talk about the cultures of spending, attitudes towards spending, people living beyond their means to keep up appearances – there are lots of those people – people not managing money on an ongoing basis, and generally, people not budgeting or managing their money properly. These people don't value or don't understand the importance of financial education, or who is actually teaching them about finance, which is a big thing.

Often, people listen to others who actually have no idea about finance. Clients will tell us about a friend who got a loan, but they have not taken into consideration their own future needs. As I said before, everybody wants money, but people have not been taught the value of actually looking after their money.

The first thing we generally do at FinanceCorp is take an assets and liabilities statement from the client, and once we actually sit with them and show them their liabilities and their earnings, quite often they realise that their liabilities are higher than or very close to their earnings. They have been wondering why they can't save anything. It is because the repayments on their debts are pretty much what they are earning. They have no idea that's the way it is because they have never actually sat down and calculated all their outgoings.

Everybody wants to have everything now; they only think about today and not tomorrow with their spending habits.

The easy availability of credit — credit cards, personal loans, car loans, boat loans — is partly to blame, but some people are also financially irresponsible. They seem to think that if the bank says they can afford it, then they can afford it. But the bank has a very limited view of what you are actually spending on a monthly basis. For example, the bank may not know exactly what you are spending on entertainment. It may be a general rule that people spend $400 a month on entertainment, but you might be spending $1,000 a month. So even though the bank might say you can afford it, you have to stop and think about whether you can actually afford it.

We always do a breakdown of monthly living expenses, and quite often it is a lot higher than the figure allocated by the bank or even what the client tells us. Most people don't realise how much money they actually spend on things. It can be things like going out for dinner or ordering takeaway. It all adds up. Their monthly shop might be higher than most other people. So instead of actually going and doing the research themselves and working out whether or not they can afford it, they just assume they can because the bank says so.

Credit cards can be a real trap. Banks regularly send out letters in the mail offering an increase on the card limit and, of course, what happens is, you think you'll get it but never use it. But then because it is there, you do use it, and increasing it again is as easy as logging on to your internet banking. There is a button you can press that actually allows you to apply for an increase to your credit card limit online.

So the banks make it quite easy for people to get into trouble with credit cards. You only have to pay 3% of the balance as a repayment, but most people don't realise that if they are only paying the minimum, they are never going to pay off the debt.

Many people are living from pay cheque to pay cheque and wondering why they never have any money. They struggle to pay down their mortgage because they are living this way. We live in a world where it's all about the image. We tend to spend money on things that will make us look good without any thought about future repercussions and how we are actually going to manage the repayments. We are keeping up with the Jones'.

Case Study

A good example is a guy working in the mines, earning $250,000 a year. He buys a boat, a jet ski, a car and everything is on finance. Then the mining industry takes a bit of a hit and he loses his job. He has to come back to Perth, where he only earns a quarter of the money, but he still has all that debt. He obviously wasn't thinking about the future, because he took out too much debt, based on an income he might not always have. That is a perfect scenario for that outcome.

A lot of people who come to us often have four or five different credit cards, with differing credit limits that are quite high, and they owe the maximum on each of them. They might also have a personal loan that they used to borrow money for a car. This happens too often.

If they get an interest-free credit card, they think that they will pay it off in 12 months, when the interest-free period is up. What they don't realise is, it is 30% on the interest, and that accumulates pretty quickly. That is when they fall behind, because they think they can pay it off in 12 months, but they don't.

Most people don't have a budget. They don't generally open a separate bank account and put money aside every pay cheque – they just don't think of doing these things. You need to set it up so that the money comes out before it hits your bank account, so you do actually save it. It is money that you never see, so there is less chance of spending it. It is little techniques like that we can help with. Struggling to get ahead can see people end up in situations where they are looking at bankruptcy, partner loans, losing their houses, or having their cars or motorbikes repossessed.

How are you going to save for a deposit when you don't even know how to? When you take on too much debt, when you buy too many things, you are never going to be able to save for a home.

If you have lots of liabilities, all your spare money goes to paying the liabilities instead of saving for a home. That is why you need that separate bank account. If you have got a home, you might not be paying down the loan because it is interest only, and instead of just doing that for 12 months, it goes on for five years. Then in five years' time you haven't actually paid anything off it, because it is an interest only loan instead of principal plus interest. You wonder why you can't find any money for a holiday or other bits and pieces, but it is because you have spent it all already. With an interest only loan, you are not going to get ahead.

We often see people taking advice from the wrong people. For example, a mate has told them to open an account in their business name. But that is not genuine savings. You need to talk to a professional who can steer you in the right direction, rather than take wrong information from people who don't actually know how the banking system works, or from people who have been there and done that.

Case Study

One of my clients is struggling a little bit with money, but he has two properties, both with a little bit of redraw in each of them. He has been told that he can take the redraw from property B and put it into property A and not have to pay any money; his interest rate or repayments won't go up on Property B. So he thought that all his problems were going to be solved because he was going to take his money from one property and put it into the other property and reduce his repayments.

Case Study *(cont.)*

The reality is that he still has to pay. The repayments are going to go up on Property B as well as down on Property A, so he is no better off for doing that. He was quite upset when he realised that was the case.

Another good example is when someone has a mortgage and a term deposit. Instead of putting the money from the term deposit into the mortgage so that it directly off-sets the mortgage and reduces the interest, they keep it in the term deposit, because they are getting 3% interest on the term deposit. But what they forget is that they are paying 4% or 5% interest on their home loan. So why would you have a term deposit that is making 3% interest, and that you are paying tax on, when you could actually have that money offsetting your mortgage at a higher interest rate?

Another scenario we often see with clients is when a friend has just consolidated all their debts into their home loan and they want to do the same thing. Or, they want to buy a house and put all their debt into it, but they've only got a 5% deposit. They don't understand why their friend was able to do it, but they can't. Most likely, their friend has got equity in their house, so there has been room to move on the mortgage.

With a lack of savings, it is easy to get into trouble if something goes wrong. A good example, again, is the guy working in the mines, having all the toys and thinking life is great. He does his two weeks on, one week off shift, has his jet-ski and boat, and then he loses his job.

These guys usually don't insure themselves, either, so he probably has no income protection, which would obviously cover him if he lost his job for a few months, depending upon the cover. He just relies on keeping his job or getting another job in the same industry that pays the same or at least similar income. But we all know that if he has to come back to the city, he is not going to get paid the same amount of money, and that is when things start to go wrong with repaying his debts. He doesn't make the repayments on the boat or the car or house, and then he is looking at losing it all. If he had been insured, things might be different.

> Often people don't know that there is a better alternative. They are not educated about anything to do with money – keeping it, spending it, insuring it. That's what we at FinanceCorp do best. We can educate you on how you should plan for the future.

Lack of knowledge results in Money Pain

Bad debt

Bad debt is pretty much anything that you don't have the money to pay for – credit cards, late payments, unsecured loans, things that don't have an asset attached to them that can be sold off and paid out. Mortgage, on the other hand, is good debt – you are paying off an asset that is going to be worth something. With bad debt, there is nothing there to help pay that debt off.

Having too many credit cards means that you are probably only going to pay 3% of the balance, and the more credit cards you've got, the more money you have to pay. So this is definitely bad debt.

Generally, once you have spent on your credit card, you can't remember what you bought, and sometimes, you start not paying off the credit card. Late payment fees get added on, and then you can't afford the interest that gets stacked on because you are not making the payments. The bank starts charging you a higher interest rate because you haven't been making your repayments.

When people can't get a loan through a normal bank, they go through one of those pay-day lenders or similar where you will mostly likely pay higher interest rates, and potentially fall further into debt. They "rob Peter to pay Paul". They'll take money out of one credit card to pay off the other credit card, and vice versa, which doesn't get them into any better position. They just get further and further into debt. Once you get to a tipping point, it can spiral out of control very quickly.

> A lot of the time, I think people spend money to feel better. After they have bought the new item, buyer remorse kicks in, and they feel bad when they realise how much they have spent. Then they just go out and do it all over again, and the cycle continues.

Culture and background can have a big impact, too. If you grew up in a family that didn't have a lot of money and relied on credit to buy things, or you haven't been taught respect for money, when you are old enough to get your first job and start earning your own money, you can quickly get into the trap of spending everything you've got, and then some, if you have a credit card.

If you haven't been taught to value money and how to make it work for you, you just continue to spend, and wonder why you never seem to have what 'everyone' else has.

Bad results

When you apply for a home loan, the bank will do what is called a credit score. If you regularly pay your bills and other debts after the due date, you are probably going to score low and be declined for a home loan because of your previous repayment history. A bad credit score can be to your detriment when you apply for a home loan, or even a personal loan.

Each bank does it differently, so it is better if you have a really good credit score, which means you don't have any defaults or late payments. Those go hand in hand with your credit score.

Key Point

Not all banks use credit scores, but most do. So if you want more options, and multiple potential lenders, then you need to have a really good credit score.

Another thing to be aware of is that mortgage insurers talk to each other. For example, say you go direct to a lender and are declined by their mortgage insurers due to your credit score. If you then go to another lender, even if they use a different mortgage insurer, the new bank is going to know that the other bank declined you, because they do talk to each other, and it will show as a credit enquiry on your credit report.

Banks either self-insure, which means they have their own sign-off for mortgage insurance, or they have an agreement with either QBE Insurance or Genworth to underwrite the loan. What does this mean? The bank might approve the loan, but the mortgage insurer might not approve your application. It is like the insurance policy on your car. The insurer is taking on your perceived risk of having a claim depending on your driving history; it is the same with Lender's Mortgage Insurer. The bank has insurance on your debt; the mortgage insurer has the final say on whether or not you get the loan, because they are the ones insuring it. Mortgage insurance is required when you don't have a 20% deposit. If you do have a 20% deposit and you've got bad debt, then you might still have a chance of getting the loan. As soon as you don't have the 20% deposit, you fall into mortgage insurance territory, and you've got less chance of getting the mortgage insurers to sign off on your application. If you're application is not signed off, you don't get the loan, or the house.

Many people still think there are 100% home loans, but they don't exist anymore. You have to have money to put towards the purchase of a house. What used to happen five or ten years ago in the mortgage industry, doesn't happen now. Things have changed.

Bad advice

A lot of parents send their children to the bank they have been with for years, and that bad advice may result in getting declined because your personal situation does not fit into the bank's assessment policy. Just because your parents got a loan from a particular bank 20 years ago doesn't mean that bank is going to give you a loan. It is no longer the

'Bank Manager' mentality, where you go into the bank and be nice to them and they give you a loan – there is a lot more involved than there used to be.

Bad advice can also come from other professionals associated with the industry. For example, real estate agents who take a cut from someone by giving biased advice or recommendations. We are not real estate agents so will never give you our 'opinion' about the value of a property. We do come across this from time to time. Occasionally, the media can be misleading or misinterpreted, because written text can be interpreted in different ways. The person giving the advice could be biased towards a particular bank, or someone who is paying to get their advertisement or name in the media.

Choosing the right people to work with is important. You don't want to go to just one bank, because they only have one product suite to offer. Similarly, if you go to a broker that only represents themselves, they don't have a group of brokers or a panel of lenders that they can work your personal scenario with.

Key Point

If you look at our model, we've got 15 brokers working together, so there are more scenarios we can all learn from. You should consider going to a broker who has been around for a while, or has someone who is a good mentor working with them. This way you can be assured you will get the best deal, tailored to suit your current and future situation.

A lot of brokers are paid commission by the lender once your application is approved and settled, so some brokers might push you towards a lender that pays them higher commission (more money). A really bad broker is someone who gives incorrect information and doesn't keep you informed about what is going on with your home loan application. This is probably the biggest issue between clients and brokers – some brokers don't communicate about what is actually going on. The broker is using the structure that suits them and delivers them more money, not what suits the client. This is not ethical or legal under current legislation.

Your mortgage broker should be someone who has had at least a couple of years' experience in lending, though not necessarily in mortgages. They should have empathy. They should also have their Certificate IV in Finance & Mortgage Broking, as well as a Diploma of Finance & Mortgage Broking Management. Not all mortgage brokers have achieved the Diploma qualification. You want someone who has completed the appropriate training and education, and someone who comes highly recommended by a friend who has already tested them. That is generally what happens for us – we are often referred by our previous clients.

Missed opportunities

An example of this kind of bad advice is taking on an interest only loan for five years because you think you can't afford it. Five years later you find you haven't actually paid anything off your loan and potentially not built any equity. That means you can't use that equity to buy another house or an investment property.

Cross-securitisation is where the bank uses one property to enable you to buy a second property. For example, let's say you have 30% equity in your owner occupier property, and you use the equity in that property to buy an investment property. You don't need to have a cash deposit to be able to purchase the second property; you just use the equity from the first. But what it means is that, for everything that happens to Property B, Property A must be used as well. If you are going to sell Property A to purchase another property, there still has to be enough equity in it to cover the debt on Property B.

Cross-securitisation means that both properties are locked in together. You might think that if you sell Property A you will be able to take $100,000 in cash from the sale. What you might not realise is that the bank might take that $100,000, or part of that $100,000, to reduce the debt on Property B to a more acceptable level.

Let's say you fund the purchase price of Property B, plus all the fees including stamp duty, conveyancing etc., through cross-securitisation, when you purchase Property B for $400,000. The debt against that property may be $425,000. When you go to sell Property A, you have got to reduce your debt, and most banks will want it reduced to 80% so that there is no lender's mortgage insurance required. You will have to reduce the debt of $425,000 to $320,000 which is 80% of $400,000 (the value of property B). You will have to use your $125,000 in equity from the sale of Property A, unless you substitute another property in.

Cross-securitisation can be a good thing, but you need to be aware of the pros and cons when you first do it. Obviously, one of the pros is that you are buying a new property. But when you buy the second property, you need to know that, prior to selling any of the properties, you should liaise again with the broker so that the figures can be worked out to make sure you can actually do it.

It is all about education and making sure that, prior to doing anything with your house or investment property, you contact your broker again. We see this mostly with investments, but people buying second homes can turn their first home into an investment. When you do something like this, there is always an element of an investment property in there.

Case Study

One of my clients had her owner-occupied home cross-securitised with four investment properties, so there were five properties involved. She'd seen a different broker for the first two properties.

Because of the way they were set up, when she sold her owner-occupied property, they were all cross-securitised. It was a nightmare, and delayed her sale. She had put her house on the market without speaking to us first. The delays cost her thousands of dollars; we had to restructure all her loans, because her structure was incorrectly set up in the first place. She had sold her owner-occupier without liaising with us about the price she needed to sell it for, or getting valuations done on the other

---

Case Study *(cont.)*
_____

properties to make sure that they could stand on their own. The properties didn't achieve the values required, therefore were not able to stand alone, and she had to pay some of the profits from the sale of her own home into her investment property loans.

If she had contacted us first, we could have advised her of all of this. The key takeaway from this is don't do anything, ever, before speaking to a quality mortgage broker.

It is always hard when those you trust, like family and friends, give you advice. You should take their advice to a professional. You are potentially going to get very different advice; some of your family and friends' advice is going to be right, and some of it is going to be wrong. If you think that it sounds right, ask a professional about it. The best thing to do is to speak with a professional first. Don't discuss it with your family and friends until you have all the information and are more educated about your home loan options. Then you can tell your family and friends, and when they come to you with their information, you are going to know what to believe and what not to believe. And if you are unsure, again, consult your broker.

Sometimes it is not necessarily bad advice or the wrong advice for the person giving it to you, but it is the wrong advice or bad advice for you. Everyone's situation is different and your friend's situation might be completely different to yours. Their broker may have said XYZ for them, but XYZ may not be good for your situation. That is why it is always good to speak to your broker. It is not so much that the information they have given you is wrong, it is just wrong for you.

'Set and forget' missed opportunities.

Quite often, clients make payments on their home loan every month and don't actually pay attention to what is going on out in the marketplace. There are promos and discounted rates available, but they think that once they have that home loan it is forever, and don't actually revisit their mortgage. They could be saving money, but they are not paying attention.

On average, most people sell their homes after about four years, so the worst case scenario is that they have a bad interest rate or a poor performing loan for four years. It used to be that people would buy a house and stay in that house forever. That's when it used to be even worse, because they wouldn't ever revisit their mortgage. Now, statistically, people are purchasing every four years, so it is not as bad as it used to be.

> ### ⊕ Key Point
>
> If you don't pay attention to your home loan, you could miss opportunities from other lenders, and you may also miss fees that you are getting charged that you shouldn't be. If you don't pay attention first up, and know that there shouldn't be an ongoing monthly fee - well, you have just paid all those repayments and could have had more money in the bank.

People with higher mortgages, say over $400,000, can save thousands over the term of their loan just by going down by half of a percent. They may not realise that such a small decrease in the interest rate can actually benefit them quite significantly. The issue is that they don't realise and they don't do the figures. They just let it sit there and forget about it.

I've had clients that were on an old product with their existing bank. They came and spoke to me, but they weren't in a position to refinance. That same bank had just released a really good product. So by coming to see me, with one email, I was able to get their interest rate reduced by over half a percent with the same bank. They didn't know that they could do that.

I've also got a client now who is paying 5.3%, and I've just had him approved for 3.99% with the same bank without refinancing. If you don't look at your mortgage every so often and you just set and forget it, then you are ripping yourself off. I was able to get him 3.99%, down from 5.3%, and he didn't have to do a thing. It was minimal work for me.

> If you are only paying the minimum repayment, you are never going to get anywhere. If you are paying the minimum and you are on an interest only loan, then you are not going have the opportunity to use your equity down the track because you are not going to have any.

People want that extra money to go out and spend on other things rather than their mortgage. Some people think it is more important to go out and have a great time, rather than paying off their mortgage. But you need to sacrifice a little bit, especially when you are younger.

When I was younger and I bought my first home, we never used to go anywhere. We were 20 years old, a time in life when most people are still out nightclubbing. But my husband and I were actually paying off two mortgages, staying home for meals, or just having a few drinks before we went out, so it didn't cost us as much when we did go out. That's what you need to do.

Even if you are paying the minimum repayment, there are different ways to do it. Instead of paying monthly, which is the standard that the banks require, if you pay your mortgage weekly or fortnightly, you are going to save on interest. Interest is calculated daily, but charged monthly. So if you are making more frequent repayments, you are still paying the same amount over the month, but you are actually reducing the interest you pay.

No future-proofing

You need to be aware that if you don't make some sacrifices now, you'll probably be working when you are 60, 70, or 80 because you are not going to have any money. That's where financial planners come into play and can do a plan for you.

⊕ Key Point

Most people don't ever think about the long term. That's why we recommend our clients see a financial planner, so that they can get educated and are not still working when they are 70. They don't worry about the 'what if'. They keep living for today. They might think about a burglary or a fire, but no further. They think of something happening, but they don't actually do anything to stop it from happening.

What happens if you do lose your job? Do you say, "Oh, I'll be right, mate. No worries." What if your partner dies or your tenants trash your house? These are the sort of things that can and do happen. In business, what happens if the market changes and what you are currently selling is no longer the trend? Well, then what are you going to sell? Insurance is the big topic here, and we are going to talk about that in the next chapter as well, but if you are not insured, and these 'what ifs' happen, well, you might be in big trouble.

Get smarter with your money

Buying a property is the biggest transaction that you are going to make in your life, yet the current generation of home buyers aren't educated on how to manage money. You are going to spend a lot of money, but you can't even handle the little bit of money that you have.

Your knowledge of mortgages and lending processes is probably very, very basic, and if you think it has no effect on you, you don't really take any interest in it. Planning for when life goes wrong is often overlooked, so you don't look at the 'what ifs' that might come down the track.

The next few chapters are going to help prevent some of the above situations from happening. I will discuss how to set yourself up for success, how to make your mortgage work for you in your current situation, and whether you need to alter your mortgage in a particular way, because sometimes life goes a bit pear-shaped.

You will learn how to ensure you get the right loan to start with, so that you get what you actually need, instead of borrowing more money and getting into more debt.

We'll discuss how to finance for investment and expansion, so taking out your mortgage now, but planning for later when you might want to buy an investment property. You are not just organising for today; you have a strategy in place.

I will show you how to plan and protect your financial future, by encouraging you to see a financial planner so that if something happens, like you lose your job or your partner dies, you are covered and things will be okay.

⊕ Key Point

You should talk to the right people before you do anything. Go and see a mortgage broker before you buy a house. But even before that, instead of putting the money into the bank and using your credit card, try actually living on the money in your wallet. It makes you more accountable for what you are spending. It makes you aware of the amount you are actually spending. Because once it's gone, it's gone.

You might think having a budget is this big, daunting exercise. Write down everything you spend in a month – put it on a piece of paper and really look at it and see how much you actually spend. That is part of having a budget, but a lot of people don't ever write down what they actually spend in a month. At the end of the month, go to your bank or credit card statement and marry the numbers up, and find out how much you really did spend on all those areas. It might be a big eye opener.

The other thing you should do is open a separate bank account. Everyone can get to their internet banking online these days, but open a separate bank account and put money into it every month, before you get paid. I recommend budgeting yourself $100 a week for spending. Also, shop online, because generally you can grab a bargain.

Never buy anything that is full-priced. Always make sure that if you are going to buy something, you buy it when it is on special. Wait for the right time to buy, instead of being impulsive. You don't always have to buy the branded peanut butter. You don't always have to buy the best. If you are buying serviettes or you are buying something that doesn't really matter, and you won't see the logo, just buy the cheapest. They are all the same at the end of the day.

If you do have a home loan, make sure you see a broker. You could be able to renegotiate your rate or refinance, and you might not even have to change banks. You might need to be set up with an offset account, so you can have your savings in your savings account, but while it is sitting there, it is offsetting your mortgage.

If you are savvy enough, you could have a credit card that you spend on, leave all your savings in your savings account, and then at the end of the month, the bank sweeps your savings account to pay off the credit card. That will ensure that you are not spending more than your wage, because the bank can't sweep if the money is not in there. I would recommend a low limit on the credit card, too; don't have a credit card limit that is more than one month's salary.

Store cards have a higher interest rate, so stick with one credit card. Don't be lured into getting multiple credit cards, because then you have multiple debts to pay off. One credit card is more than enough.

Take responsibility for your own money. Just because you get a letter in the mail, or your bank or someone else says they will give you more money, that's not necessarily a good thing.

> Having a better lifestyle is not about getting a bigger credit card limit. It is about working smarter and harder, being educated and making smart investments, starting a business, getting a promotion, getting a second job – a lot of people do these sorts of things. Typically, the more money you earn, the more you spend.

Key takeaways

This chapter was about education – making sure that you talk to the right people, plan for your future and work with a trusted team of people to point you in the right direction. It was also about good debt versus bad debt and what that means, and it offered some tips on how not to get into a bad situation, or worry about keeping up with the Jones'.

It is all about education. You need to educate yourself by talking to professionals, not your friends and family.

It is great to Google for information and to read books, but if it is not specific to your particular scenario, then you could be reading the wrong stuff. It is more important to get into a good spending routine and talk to the right people. You have got to find someone you trust. If you don't trust them and the rapport just isn't there, then you are not going to be 100% sure that they are doing the right thing for you. Maybe you know other people that have used them before and had good experiences, but it is about finding someone you trust.

Think before you do something and think of the future you – think about you in 10, 20, 30, 40 years' time and give that guy or girl a break.

CHAPTER 2

How to make your mortgage work for you

In the previous chapter, we talked about the importance of having a good attitude towards managing your money in a smart way and thinking about your future so that you can avoid financial pain down the track. We discussed how to avoid making mistakes and listening to the wrong people. So this chapter is for people who already have a mortgage, but we are also going to talk about the mortgage process for people that are interested in buying their first property as well.

I am going to give you an overview of the mortgage process – what happens and when it happens. Everyone's situation is different, so we need the most suitable solution for that particular client. I'll show you some mistakes to avoid, things that might alert you to what can happen before it happens, how to pay your mortgage off faster so you can have the financial freedom that we spoke about earlier, and why you need to work with a professional adviser. I can point you in the right direction so that you, too, can get ahead in life.

Mortgage process

The mortgage process is all about getting your finances in order. Obviously, you need to save some money. First, look at what you are spending and get an idea of how much you can actually save, and make sure that your current payments are in order with your credit cards, personal loans, and car loans. Even your phone and utility bills can impact your credit score if they are not paid on time. You also need to speak to a mortgage broker about staying on track with your spending habits, how much you need as a deposit, and what sort of paperwork you need to get together. This is the first step.

Valuable Resource

You can get a free credit check by going online to www.veda.com.au, or you can contact a mortgage broker. Most mortgage brokers can do a credit check, so it's not diffi cult to get an idea of your current credit score.

If you think you might not have a good credit rating, there are credit agencies or lawyers who can look into your defaults. If the agency that put the default on your credit file hasn't completed all the steps correctly, there are lawyers who can get those removed for you. It also depends how long the default has been there. If it has been there for six and a half years and has been paid, you might have to wait six months before you can apply for a loan, because by then it will have dropped off, which will increase your score. A low credit score is not a good thing.

Key Point

You should open a bank account in the same name as the mortgage holder. Don't put your savings in mum and dad's bank account. Put it in your own personal account. The account needs to have your name on it, and it needs to show genuine savings. You also need to be putting money into that savings account on a regular basis and not making any withdrawals.

Another option to consider is a guarantor loan. If you don't have enough savings, your parents can put up their property as security as long as they have got at least 40% equity in that property. They need to have 20% equity to avoid mortgage insurance, and then they need to give you 20% of their equity as well. Basically, the title of your parent's house goes back to the bank if they don't have a mortgage on it. If they do have a mortgage, then your bank will take a second mortgage on the property.

You don't have to go to the same bank that your parents have their home loan with. Some lenders won't allow second mortgages, so then you might have to use the same bank. But if the lender does allow other banks to take a second mortgage, then that is okay. Just be aware that, at any stage, a bank can refuse a second mortgage; it is not a given that the bank will allow it.

Getting your finances in order means saving up enough of a deposit, or getting access to enough for a deposit. The minimum is 2% if you are a first home buyer in Western Australia. In other states it is 5% in genuine savings. You may also need a few thousand dollars for mortgage insurance, depending on which lender you use. Not all banks will add the entire mortgage insurance on to the loan; some may want it paid up front.

Case Study

For example, for a $400,000 loan, you'd need a $20,000 deposit, about $3,000 for fees and then roughly 1% for mortgage insurance as well, which would be about $4,000. So that comes to about $27,000 on a $400,000 property. Most of the mortgage insurance can be capitalised, but it's best to allow for it on top, just in case. At a 95% lend, lender's mortgage insurance (LMI) will normally take the loan amount up to 98% of the purchase price. Most lenders will only lend up to 97%, capping the LMI, so then you have to make up the short fall, approximately 1%. The fees you will pay include conveyancing or settlement agent fees, land and water rates, and any government fees as well.

Western Australia is similar to the other states. The conveyancing would be about the same and land rates would be much of a muchness. We always over estimate, so $3,000 for fees is probably around $500 over what you need; but it's better to overestimate and receive a bonus at the end than to underestimate and have to come up with money that you don't have.

If you are trying to figure out how much you need to save, it's around 7% of the purchase price in total. That is for first home buyers. There are different regulations in each state. In Western Australia, there is no stamp duty as long as you purchase a property under $430,000. Between $430,000 and $530,000 there is a pro-rata rate. If you are purchasing vacant land, the vacant land purchase price needs to be $300,000 or less to avoid stamp duty.

If your state doesn't have stamp duty concessions, you are going to have to save the 5% deposit plus stamp duty, or 7% plus stamp duty, which varies from state to state. We always work on about 10%, being 5% for fees and 5% for the deposit. So on a $400,000 property; you need about $40,000, worst case scenario.

The most important thing is to speak to a professional first to see what is relevant in your state or territory.

In Western Australia, we have a state government incentive called Keystart, and they are funded by the state government. They are not a bank. They only require a 2% deposit. There is no lender's mortgage insurance, but there are other things that go with that, as well. Of your 2% deposit, 1% needs to come from genuine savings over a three-month period. The other 1% can come from anywhere. The fees are normally about $1,500 just for the bank, and then you need to have your settlement agent fees on top of that as well. There is no mortgage insurance payable.

Once you've got your finances in order, we email you a template of all the things that we require before you come to the actual appointment.

These include:

$ a colour copy of your driver's licence, back and front

$ a passport or birth certificate

$ a letter of confirmation of employment (that is generally to say that you are not on probation)

$ your two most recent payslips, no more than 30 days old

$ your last group certificate – if you are self-employed we need two years' tax returns

$ bank statements confirming deposits

$ three months' history of genuine savings

$ most recent six months of mortgage statements, dated in the last 30 days if you are refinancing

$ copies of your credit card statements for the last three months

$ a rate notice if you are refinancing

$ a copy of all the pages of the offer of acceptance if you are purchasing

$ a rental letter/lease agreement from investment properties

$ a gift letter, if applicable

$ copy of permanent residency or visa sheet of passport, if applicable

$ a current Centrelink statement outlining family tax benefits you receive

$ ABN showing declared income, if applicable

$ a breakdown of your monthly living expenses, e.g. insurance, housekeeping, food, phone, internet, etc

The gift letter is normally a Statutory Declaration or Stat Dec, as they are known. The Stat Dec should say that the money you are receiving is a gift and is non-repayable. If you have to pay it back, then the lender needs to take that repayment into consideration as well, because that is really another liability that you have.

We need your driver's licence and passport to verify that you are who you say you are.

If you are on probation at your current workplace, the bank needs to know that, so the confirmation of employment letter needs to show how long you have been employed and your current income. That is generally required. If you can't provide payslips with dates on them, you may be able to use salary credits to your bank account. By law, you are supposed to have payslips, but there are alternatives. A group certificate (or payment summary, as they are now known) is pretty self-explanatory. If you are paid on a commission basis, the lender might ask for the group certificate, because then they can see what you have earned in previous years and get an idea of your regular income source.

Your bank statement confirming three months' deposit history proves that you have been making regular deposits. You can't just put money in and draw it out straightaway – there has got to be a snowball effect. They have got to see it grow without too many withdrawals. Bank statements are sometimes required to make sure that you do not have any undeclared debts or spending behaviours that might be considered risky by the banks. If you are refinancing, six months of mortgage statements will suffice to confirm that payments have been on time every month. If we are looking to consolidate your credit cards into your mortgage, lenders will use your credit card statements to confirm repayments have been on time and that you have no risky spending habits.

The rates notice is used to confirm you are living at the property declared as your principal place of residence, the bank will also check that rates has been paid on time and that there are no outstanding amounts due. These methods of verification are used to prove to the lender that you are of good financial character.

The offer of acceptance, or contract of sale, is to outline many things – purchase price, finance due date, settlement date, the terms and conditions of contract, and any other special terms you might request be included in the contract.

If you are buying an investment property and you don't currently have a lease agreement in place, the agent can provide a letter confirming the proposed rental. However, if you already have an investment property, and you have a lease agreement in place, the bank will use the lease to confirm rental income. Another method of confirming rental income is through a valuation.

Proof of your permanent residency is required for first home buyers, because you can't get the first home buyers' grant unless you are a permanent resident of Australia.

Centrelink paperwork is required if you are using family tax A and B to assist your affordability. We need to be able to confirm what entitlement you are receiving. With regard to that, if your children are over 11, some lenders will pro rata the benefit amount allowed for servicing. The reason for this is, if the loan is taken over a 30-year term, you will not be receiving those benefits for the entire term of the loan.

The last one, a breakdown of your monthly expenses. This will show what you are spending on general day-to-day living.

If you are employed on a casual basis, most banks need to see continuous employment for at least 12 months; however, there are some banks that will accept just three months. If you are a permanent part-time employee, they will accept all the income, and some banks, depending upon the loan valuation, will accept one day in the job as long as you have a pay slip. Others might be more stringent and say you have to have been in the job for three months or six months before they'll accept that income.

That's why using a mortgage broker is beneficial, because we'll know which banks will accept your income and how much of it, as well. Banks tend not to like causal employment; they prefer you to have a permanent part time or full time job.

> ### Key Point
> You can still get a loan if you are casually employed, you just have limits on which banks you can go through to get your loan. Casual could also mean contract. You could be up in the mines earning $80,000 a year, but that is still casual work.

Using a mortgage broker

A broker has a panel of lenders all offering different products. As brokers it is our job to understand the different bank policies. Going from one bank to another and getting rejected negatively impacts your credit score. Reputable brokers offer more options, more lenders, and you will not ruin your credit score. Be sure to ask a real estate agent, financial planner, family members and friends if they can recommend a good broker.

We work for you, our client. We act as the intermediary between the bank and the client, doing all the running around, following up with the bank and keeping everyone up to date on the application progress. The best part for our clients is that we are paid for all of our time and experience by the banks. Our clients benefit without having to pay the bill.

The first thing we do as your broker is take a 'fact find' over the phone, which includes your full name, address, income, how long you have been working there, your assets and liabilities. From all that information we can see if you meet the banks' policies, if you have enough for a deposit, and if you can afford it, because really, those are the three most important things. If you don't fit the criteria or tick all the boxes, then we will send you an email with some information on finance, and tell you what you need to do. Then we follow up with you after a month, or two months, or three months, as advised in our email.

We have a serviceability calculator for each bank. We type in your income and your liabilities and it tells us how much you can afford. That is another good reason to use a broker, because we can go to all the different banks that have a calculator, and we can get you more money if you need it. The amount you can borrow could vary by as much as $20,000 to $30,000, because they all use different parameters for assessment.

The banks have different assessment rates – what the bank assesses you can afford to repay. So, as an example, the interest rate from one lender might be 4.04%, but the assessment rate for that lender is 7.25%. That means they assess what you could afford to borrow if the interest rate were 7.25%.

This safeguards you, so that if there are interest rate rises through the Reserve Bank of Australia (RBA) that are passed on, you are not going to be in a position where, after one or two rate rises, you're going to be in financial hardship. It is the bank's way of stress testing your financial position and making sure that they don't lend you more than you can actually afford to repay.

The other variable is your living expenses. Different banks use different systems. One of these is the Henderson Poverty Index. This index uses the average cost of living, irrespective of income, for the average single person or couple, with or without dependent children. There is another system, known as HEM (Household Expenditure Measure) that is based on what you earn. Using this system, the assumption is based on the more you earn, the more your basic livings costs are. Previously, all banks used the Henderson Poverty Index, but now many banks have moved towards HEM.

Case Study

As an example, if you went with Keystart Home Loans, and they agreed to lend you about $200,000, you would probably get $250,000 or $260,000 from a bank like the Commonwealth Bank of Australia (CBA), because Keystart don't lend a lot of money. But you only need a 2% deposit with Keystart. So there could be a variance between the CBA and Westpac, where the CBA might loan you $250,000, but Westpac might loan you $270,000 under the same scenario. It happens quite a bit, which is why we do refinancing. If you can't afford what you want with one bank, we refinance you elsewhere so you can get more money and better products.

The borrowing calculators you find on websites are very generic. They have a generic assessment rate and generic living expenses. Obviously there is no way to include every single bank's assessment rate and living expenses. An online calculator is going to give you an indication of approximately how much you can borrow. They don't work well for self-employed people, who may not put in their taxable income, but rather the cash they have received. They may have made $90,000 for the year, but their taxable income may only be $25,000. That is going to give them the wrong borrowing capacity, because they have used the wrong income. At the time of writing, it is the banks' policy to only use 80% of overtime earnings. If you entered your total overtime income into one of these generic calculators, the result will be a false borrowing capacity. People often forget to put in all their debts – remember these are generic and are not designed to take all scenarios into account.

Another thing to consider is that if you were to make a loan application enquiry online through one of the banks websites, this may show as a credit enquiry on your credit file. Similarly, if you do this on a broker's website, there is also a chance this could happen. It is not always the case, however. We don't conduct a credit enquiry on our website.

⊕ Key Point

Most people don't realise that if they fill out a credit card application for say Bankwest, and it gets declined, and then they do one with Westpac, and then with CBA, every time they do one, it puts an enquiry on their credit file, even if it has been declined. This will affect your credit score.

There is a very complex algorithm used to determine a credit score. Basically a number or score is allocated to everything in your application. If you have numerous enquiries on your credit report, then that reduces your score. The more enquiries that are on your credit report, the less likely you are to make a successful loan application.

Quite often banks will say your application has been declined because it doesn't credit score very well and they won't give you an exact reason. However, the most likely reason will be a large number of enquiries on your credit report.

All the banks can see that you have made multiple credit applications and unless you have a good reason, even if they don't check your credit score, they are going to want to know why all the other banks have declined, or why you haven't gone with the other banks.

As I mentioned earlier, you should also be careful about blindly trusting a bank's assessment of how much you can afford to borrow. For example, the bank might say that, based on your income, you can borrow $1,000,000, but you need to have the right deposit in order to do that in the first place. It would also mean that the repayments are quite high, even though the bank thinks you can afford it, you need to work out what the repayments are and put it into a budget to make sure that you can actually afford it without sacrificing too much of your leisure time activity.

There is another consideration when deciding the loan amount you can comfortably afford. If your budget is already struggling, and interest rates go up to 17%, this could be financially catastrophic. Naturally, the higher the interest rate, the higher the repayments. When it comes to borrowing capacity, a broker can help to assess your needs after completing a simple fact find process.

Pre-approval

The next step in the process, after we get all the information from you, all your documents, is to lodge it with a bank. The bank then does a credit check, verifies your income by looking at your payslips, makes sure that it all definitely fits their policy and, if so, issues a pre-approval or conditional approval.

Key Point

It is important to get a pre-approval, because although the broker might think that the bank will accept that income, they may not. So instead of just doing our homework, once we select the bank, we submit it to make sure that everything sits okay with the bank.

Remember, it is not just the bank that is approving your application; it is also the mortgage insurer in some instances. If your application falls into mortgage insurance territory, the bank is going to scrutinise the application more than if it doesn't require mortgage insurance.

If you need a mortgage-insured loan, you definitely need to submit your loan application to the bank before you go shopping. You might be unaware of a default on your file, and think it is all good. But by submitting the loan application, that will be picked up, and could knock it on the head straight away.

One of the biggest mistakes we see people make when saving for a home is putting money into a parent's bank account. That is a big no-no. Another is changing your current employment, even when you have a pre-approval. Let's say you are currently working full time with a recruitment agency, and your employer decides to change you to casual. That can affect your application.

You might put in an offer on a house before speaking to us and you then find that you can't afford that house, or may not have enough deposit to buy that house; that is another mistake, as is accidently letting your credit card go into default. That comes up a lot.

You might be saving your money and doing really well, putting money in regularly, but then you take it back out, which just resets that whole three months of genuine savings. You could have a tax debt to pay; that sometimes knocks it on the head.

People tend to lend other people money out of their savings, and when they get it back, it is no longer classed as genuine savings. They also sometimes check their borrowing capacity using the bank's online calculator and think they are right to go. Then they put in an offer, and unfortunately, we have to tell them that they can't actually borrow that much money. They trust the bank's online calculator, or they trust what a friend says about buying a property, and they assume they are right. Maybe they think they can borrow 100% of the purchase price, so they put an offer in, and then they come to us and we tell them that there are no more 100% loans. They might think that they can get $3,000 if they are a first home buyer, but that may not be true.

The worst outcome of these kinds of mistakes is that you lose the property. You put an offer in and get all excited, and think you are going to get it, and when we can't get the finance you become disheartened. If you had come to us first, we could have advised you and you wouldn't have wasted time putting in an offer. Another possible outcome is having to go to an alternate lender because you haven't got enough deposit, or don't fit the bank's policy.

On the eastern seaboard, auctions are the popular way to buy property, and with auctions, generally you've got to have your finance sorted before you go. You bid on the day, and if you win the bid and buy the property and you can't come up with the money, you can be sued. So really, with an auction, you need to talk to the bank, use the equity in your home, and get a line of credit so that you have the money sitting there ready to pay for it. A lot of people don't realise that an auction is like a cash offer, and they also don't realise that you have to pay a 10, 20 or 30% deposit on the day. You need to have access to those funds straight away.

You need to get pre-approval before you fall in love with a house, otherwise the loan could be declined. Banks can take up to 28 days to process your application, so you need to give yourself enough time for the process to go smoothly.

Making an offer

When you are ready to make an offer, talk to a real estate agent, assuming that you have already spoken to a broker and have a pre-approval in place. The real estate agent will take your offer to the owners of the property to see if they are happy with the price and the times for finance and settlement dates. If there are any requirements that the buyers have put in the contract, such as a particular item is to stay, they also make sure that the sellers are happy with the added conditions. If they are not happy with the price or something in the contract, then negotiation takes place between the real estate agent, the buyer and the seller.

Once they all agree on a price and all the conditions, the contract is signed off and accepted, and it becomes a legal, binding contract. There are generally only three things that can cause a contract to fall over:

$ the contract is subject to finance and the finance falls through

$ the contract is subject to a pest inspection and the property doesn't pass the pest inspection

$ the contract is subject to a building inspection and the property doesn't pass the building inspection

However, if the finance is pre-approved, then that means that the contract can go ahead, subject to all other conditions being met. It then becomes a live contract and you have bought the house.

So, in order for the transaction to go smoothly, you need to talk to the broker to find out how long you need for finance and how long for settlement on the contract. You need to make sure that you get all the documents to the mortgage broker so that if the bank requests more information, they are on the ball and can provide all the information as soon as possible. The real estate agent needs to make sure that when the bank wants to do an evaluation it can be done straight away, and that it goes smoothly. Also, with regard to settlement, we need to make sure that you sign the mortgage documents correctly and the settlement agency documents quickly in order for the settlement to go through on time. Normally it takes 28 days for finance and 28 days for settlement in Perth, but in the eastern states, it is normally two weeks for finance and two weeks for settlement, so it is pretty quick.

Settlement can be delayed if the bank takes longer than expected, or doesn't issue the documents correctly and they need to be redone. In that case, we have to get an alteration to the contract. So sometimes we have to rearrange things, and if you are late, the vendor or the buyer can charge you penalties. That is another reason it is important to make sure that things go smoothly, because it could cost you money.

Unless you are paying cash and have the money in the bank, the contract is always subject to finance, and it is generally 28 days. If the real estate agent wants confirmation that you have actually put a pre-approval in to the bank, then you should give them your mortgage broker's details.

Approval

If you are a first home buyer, we need to send off your First Home Buyer Grant application form and make sure that is processed and approved, and generally, that is when the pest inspection is done. Then the loan documents are issued to you and the mortgage broker will help sign you up. Alternatively, you can go into the branch and the staff will help you sign your mortgage documents and send them off. It is imperative that you get the documents done quickly and send them back as soon as possible.

You must also organise insurance for the property – building insurance – and send that to the bank. The mortgage broker will follow this up. You'll also have settlement documents that need to be signed and sent back to the settlement agent. Once all the paperwork is signed for the settlement and the mortgage, and you have insurance, then the settlement agent will liaise with the bank to book settlement. Once settlement occurs, your repayments will start weekly, fortnightly or monthly after the settlement date.

Once you start making repayments, make sure they are on time. Get used to having your mortgage repayment there instead of paying rent, which is normally higher. You should try to put extra money into your mortgage, whether it is an extra $10 or $20 dollars a week or a month, any extra cash. If you put that straight into your mortgage, with most banks, you can access it as a redraw on their mortgage. Then, if you do get into financial hardship, you have the extra money you paid into your mortgage to guard against late payments.

⊕ Key Point

There is another benefit to paying that little bit extra – let's just say that your principal and interest repayment is $500 a week. You can increase that with the bank and make it $550 a week. So then you are effectively saving $200 a month without even knowing about it, because it just comes out with the repayment.

When it comes to home loans, one size doesn't fit all. Make sure you choose a loan with the features and benefits that are right for you. We can recommend a loan for your particular needs – and take care of all the paperwork. When you're ready, talk to us to discuss next steps.

How to get ahead

Who is going to provide for your future if you haven't got your house paid off and have investments and enough super? Is there going to be a pension? Is it going to be enough? Maybe?

You might not get a pension when you are older, so that is something that you need to think about. Superannuation? Will that be enough to support you moving forward? If you don't think it will be, then you need to put extra money into your super, which most people don't think about, because they only think about today.

Will the family home be big enough? If you are paying extra on your mortgage, you are building equity quicker. You might only have one child now, but moving forward you might have two or three. If you are making extra repayments on your house, you will build equity quicker, so then you have options if the house does get too small, and you can move on and buy something else. Otherwise, you could be stuck in the same small house and just have to live with it because you don't have enough equity.

Also, how will you support your family in the future? Are you always going to work? When do you want to stop working? You need a financial plan that says, "Right, by the time I'm 55, I'm going to stop working and

I'm going to have $300,000 in super."You need to think about not just today, but the future, too.

Do you know how much is enough?

Well, when you get a financial plan done by talking to a financial planner, you'll know the answer to that question. We'll discuss this further in later chapters. A financial planner will do a plan for you, so you know what you need to do. But then you also need to stick to it and keep that strategy moving forward. As well as a financial planner, the other person that I would probably talk to is an accountant, especially if you have your own business. You need to talk to the accountant and the financial planner so they can give you the long term view of what you need to do. Obviously, you need to stick to it, which is often the hardest part.

> My best tip for sticking to your plan is to write it down and revisit it every week or every month, minimum, and see how you are going. You could also put it up on the wall or somewhere it will be constantly visible.

A financial planner has a duty of care to call you every 12 months to see how you are going. But if you wait for your planner to check up on you, 12 months is way too long. Lots of things can happen in 12 months, and the problem is that most people do wait that long, which is not a good thing.

You should set up a reminder in your calendar to check on your finances every month. You should also set up a direct debit, or change your monthly repayments. Instead of paying $500, make it $550. Ask your workplace to take an extra $50 a week out of your pay cheque and put it into your super. If you can do those sorts of things so you don't see the money, you're not in control of it and it just happens, then that is what you need to do. Then you need to have your yearly update.

A lot of people will spend money if they have it in the bank, whereas if they don't see it, they don't spend it.

If you want to pay off your mortgage quicker, as I said, arrange with your bank to make a higher repayment than what is required. That will give you that financial freedom earlier, so you won't have to pay the mortgage off over 30 years. You will build equity quicker, and you won't notice the difference because you have always done it this way.

You could also utilise an off-set account. All your savings go into the offset account. Every day that the money is sitting there, it is offsetting your mortgage. Generally, you must have a minimum of $1,000 or $2,000 in the offset account, but some banks have no minimum. Using this feature could reduce your loan term and the amount of interest you will pay.

You can also make all your payments on your credit card, leave all your money in your offset/savings account, and then every month, get the bank to do a sweep and pay off the credit card in full with the money that is in your offset/savings account. Doing all of these things will get you ahead much quicker. It works this way:

⊕ Key Point

Interest is calculated daily and charged to your account monthly. So every day that the money is sitting in your savings account it is off-setting your mortgage. By having your pay come in on the 1st of the month and leaving it in your offset account all month while you pay for things on a credit card, for those 30 days you are offsetting the interest by that amount, but not accruing any interest on the credit card. Credit cards usually have an interest-free period of 55 days. If you pay it off every 30 days, there is no interest charged.

Obviously, the more you earn, the more impact this is going to have, but it could probably reduce the term of a home loan by 5 or 10 years. That's how I paid off my house.

Another way to get ahead faster is to pay the principal and interest instead of interest only. With an interest only loan of 5 years, in 5 years' time you are still going to owe the same amount of money, because all you are doing is paying the interest. With a principal and interest loan, you are reducing the principal and interest. So you are going to pay your house off over the 30 years, whereas with interest only, your loan balance never reduces and you'll always be in debt to the bank. When your interest only period expires, you will only have 25 years to pay off the full amount of the loan plus interest.

If you have credit cards, find ones with the lowest interest rate. A lower interest rate equals more cash flow because the repayments are lower. You can refinance your credit cards, but how many times do you want to refinance? Just pay them off.

That's also another way of reducing what you have to pay on your mortgage – refinance. Get a better rate and still make the same repayment as before, because that is going to reduce the loan quicker. Always keep in touch with your broker and make sure you are on a great deal, as that can also save you money and get you ahead faster.

The broker will know if they can get you a better rate. Sometimes when you are in mortgage insurance territory, there is no point moving to a better rate, because you have to repay your mortgage insurance. So talk to your broker before you apply and don't waste your time and potentially your money. Your broker can tell you whether it is going to work or not.

⊕ Key Point

If you are making weekly payments instead of fortnightly or monthly, you are reducing your principal quicker, which is also reducing your interest payments. The more often you pay into your home loan, the more interest you are going to save.

There is another way to get ahead that we haven't discussed yet and it has to do with the equity you have in your property. Once you have owned your property for a while, you can use the equity you have as leverage to borrow again and purchase another property as an investment. We'll be talking about this in the next chapter.

Who are you working with?

You must understand the importance of enlisting the help of professionals.

The first port of call is the mortgage broker who will look at your current situation and make sure that you are pointed in the right direction, which we spoke about before. Alongside that, if you are self-employed, you need to talk to your accountant to get your financials, so they are probably the second person you should talk to. From there, you need a real estate agent to find the right property for you based on how much you can afford, your budget and what you are looking for in a property.

The deal will be submitted to the bank so they can do their due diligence and evaluation. Once the loan is approved, you need to send off the unconditional approval to a conveyancing solicitor or settlement agent. The settlement agent prepares the settlement documents. At the same time, you need to talk to an insurance broker or insurance company to get your new house building covered. If something were to happen and it burnt down, you wouldn't be left with just the land; you would be able to rebuild and have a house to live in.

So that is the process and, obviously, a mortgage broker will see you through all those processes and hold your hand.

It is important to keep in touch with your mortgage broker even after you have bought your property to make sure that you are still on a competitive rate and that you are heading in the right direction, or even to find out if you have enough equity to buy an investment property. Also, if you see that fees are being charged and they shouldn't be, you should be chatting to your mortgage broker to find out why.

Mortgage brokers have all the up to date information. We know what is happening in the industry, what we can and can't do, and the correct process. We can ensure you are doing the right thing legally. We've got access to products and markets, and we can provide you with information so that you can read and educate yourself.

We take the hard work out of the process, and eliminate the complexity and make it stress-free for you. We find the best choices for our clients and make sure you are heading in the right direction, because the cheapest is not always the best. We'll match your current situation with the right options. And we can tailor the options for certain circumstances to avoid costly mistakes, as well.

> ### ⊕ Key Point
>
> I want to reiterate the importance of using professionals. People talk to friends or look at something online and think they are an expert, but there is so much more to getting a home loan and buying a property than you might think.

Key takeaways

It is most important to connect with the right people and engage a mortgage broker to see you through the process, but you should also get the right mortgage broker – not every broker knows their stuff. Dealing with the right people throughout the process is really, really important so make sure that you keep in touch with everybody.

You need to look forward to what you've got happening in the future as well, and make sure that you know what you are doing. Once you have purchased your property, you want to pay it off as quickly as possible using the tips we've discussed – by making extra payments, utilising an offset account or a credit card, and paying your mortgage weekly instead of monthly, because all of these things will save you a lot of money.

CHAPTER 3

Investing in your future

When considering your future, buying a second home as an investment property is probably the most popular thing to do. Once you have an investment property, you can build equity in it and use that to buy another property. Most people also use their owner-occupied home, which holds most of the equity, to cross-collateralise and buy something else. Or you could buy commercial properties.

If you buy an investment property, you can stay in your job and lease it out, or you could do what we call a business expansion. Business expansion could mean buying a commercial property and instead of renting it out, using it for your own business. Or it could mean borrowing money to expand your business, because not everyone has enough cash flow or cash upfront to do so. For example, if you already own one franchise cake shop, you might buy another and have two franchises.

Equipment finance is another form of investment. You could expand your business by buying bigger machinery which allows you to expand and diversify so you can produce other things and make more money.

And lastly, buying properties through a Self-Managed Super Fund (SMSF) also seems to be more popular now. You can buy residential or commercial property using an SMSF, and although there are lots of laws and legalities around that, it is definitely worth considering as an investment opportunity.

> ### ⊕ Key Point
>
> In order to buy your second home, the best scenario is to have at least 30 percent equity in your current property, so that you do not need mortgage insurance. A lot of people buying investment property pay mortgage insurance and that may be claimable on tax. Most people do it to reduce their taxable income, which is called negative gearing.

To buy a commercial property you generally need at least 30% of the purchase price plus fees, so roughly 40% equity in your current property or in cash. For a business expansion, the deposit could be $20,000 or more. If you want to invest millions, you have got to have at least a 20% or 30% deposit, maybe more, and if you want to buy a franchise, you generally need a 40% deposit to invest in one.

If you are using your SMSF, you can generally borrow around 70% of the purchase price for a commercial property, and sometimes up to 80%, depending upon the lender. If you are buying a residential property, I believe it is about 80%, again, depending on which lender you use. So you need to have 20% or 30% deposit plus your fees in your SMSF. You also need to be making regular contributions into your super fund; otherwise you won't get finance for the property.

The good thing about buying an investment property is that you're generally building equity if you are making extra payments on it. But if interest rates go up, the rent you are getting might not cover as much, so you might have to make extra payments just to meet the monthly repayment. It's the same with commercial properties.

There are a couple of positives to owning a commercial property – you don't have to pay for regular inspections because you don't have to do them as often, and generally the lease is for five years, whereas residential leases are usually for only six or twelve months. Tenants are locked into a commercial property for a longer term, so it is kind of set and forget for a while. The other positive to a commercial property investment is that the tenant pays all the outgoings, such as strata fees and any over and above costs. With a residential property, you have to pay the water supply charges and the tenant has to pay the water usage charges. The negative side of owning commercial property is that if you put in a tenant that you don't like, and they are on a five-year lease, you are stuck with them for five years.

Business expansion can help you make more money, but you also take on more debt. If you expand and it doesn't work, then you could be in trouble. On the other hand, if you expand and it does work, then you could be a multi-millionaire. So there is good and bad to consider. Equipment finance generally goes hand in hand with your expansion. You are buying more equipment so you can expand your business, so if something goes wrong with the equipment and it needs to be fixed, it can be quite costly. But if you don't have the equipment, you are not going to be able to increase your cash flow.

SMSF's are great if you haven't got the cash up front. You can take your deposit from your SMSF and grow your portfolio for when you retire. The downside of using your SMSF is that the house or property you purchase has to stay in there; you can't cross-collateralise. It is a stand-alone security, so once you pay it off, you can't then use the equity you have to buy another property. Plus, all the money you receive from the house has to go into the SMSF, so you don't actually get to utilise that money or spend it to buy something else.

Buying your second home or an investment property

Often people will say they want to buy another house for themselves and make their current house an investment property, and that is well and good, but they want to know whether they have to sell it. Well, that will depend on the equity you have in it. It also depends on how much you owe, because if you want to negatively gear it, then it might be better for you to sell it. I would advise you to speak to an accountant about what is best for your financial situation. We can give you the figures, too, about whether you have enough equity and cash and whether it is a good idea to keep your current home. But you really need to talk to an accountant, as well.

The bank will look at your financial situation and include your rental income, because obviously, you are going to be renting it out, and that helps with serviceability or your ability to afford the loan. But other than that, they look at it exactly the same way whether you are buying your first house or your second house. As long as you can afford it, you have the deposit and you fit the bank's policy, they're the main things the bank is looking for. You can use the equity in your current house and either top up your current loan, or take the cash and do a stand-alone investment loan. That way, the two loans aren't together at the same bank, which makes it easier if you want to sell one later. You can also cross-collateralise, which means the bank will take both properties as security, but if you want to sell one, you need to make sure that the one that the bank is keeping has enough equity in it, and that is up to the bank to decide. Generally, it is around 10% or 20% equity.

⊕ Key Point

Of all these approaches, I would recommend the stand-alone option. It's best not to have them cross-collateralised because if you want to sell one, the bank needs to do an evaluation on the other property. Then they have the say on how much money you have to put in to the loan that remains. When you have a stand-alone loan, you can just sell it, and as long as the bank gets all their money back, they are happy.

It's really a good idea not to top up your current loan for the second property purchase. Yes, you will have only one payment, but when it comes to tax time, you can only claim the interest on your investment property, so you need to have the two loans separate. A good broker will be aware of things like that.

Keeping your loans separate will assist your accountant to work out the interest you are paying on the investment loan. This is really, really, really, important. Should you stay with the same bank? You can, but I would still have two separate loans. I would probably recommend you have them with different banks if you can, so you don't have all your eggs in one basket. If one bank decides to up their rates by 2%, it doesn't affect 100% of your investment portfolio. If the bank changes their policy, then you've only got one loan with them instead of two, so I think it is better to have them split between different banks.

If you have a mortgage on your owner-occupied property, then you should almost always have your investment property on an interest only loan, because you can claim the interest on your investment property against your tax, but not on your own home. You want to pay your own home loan down faster because you can't claim that, whereas the investment property you can. Obviously, with these sorts of strategies, you need to speak to your accountant.

Negative gearing is when you have a $2,000 repayment to make, for example, and your rent only comes to $1,800. In that scenario, your property is negatively geared by $200 because the rent falls short of the repayment amount. If it is positive, your repayment might be $2,000, and the rent you are receiving is $2,200, so you are getting a positive payment of $200. Whether your property is negatively or positively geared depends on the strategy you are trying to achieve. Again, that is something the accountant needs to comment on.

If you buy a property in an area where you can get really good rent and it doesn't cost a lot, the repayments can be quite affordable. For instance, in Kwinana in Western Australia, you could buy a nice four-bedroom, two-bathroom house for around $300,000 and the repayments would be around $1,200 a month (at current interest rates). But if you were getting $1,100 or $1,200 a month in rent, the only reason you would have to put money to it would be if the property was not leased, or if something went wrong with the property. You would be paying interest only on the loan, so if the rent covered the repayments and you could put a few thousand dollars away for rent and bits and pieces, that's how you could afford to repay the loan. At tax time, if it is negatively geared, you might actually get money back on your tax as well. Then you have just got to hope that the market goes up, because the more equity you build, the better off you are going to be.

There are several ways to increase your cash flow. You could get a higher paying job, charge more rent on your investment property, and you could spend less. If you have an investment property and you want to get ahead, you need to cut down on your spending, and pay more off your owner-occupied home, as well as pay your mortgage weekly instead of monthly. All those things will increase your cash flow.

Bridging finance can be arranged for the situation where you have your house on the market and you find another house that you really like and want to put in an offer on, but you want to take the other house off the market. The only way to do this, if you haven't sold your own house, is to get what we call bridging finance. This means that you will have six months to sell your house before the bank requires you to make payments on either your current house or your new house.

Key Point

Bridging finance allows you to make an offer and take the house that you love off the market before you sell the property you are currently living in. I don't recommend this to clients at all because you could end up paying interest only on two properties if you can't sell your property. The bank only gives you six months where you don't have to make any repayments, but you still are paying interest on the loans, so it is actually getting you further in debt.

My recommendation is not to do bridging loans. If you own your current house outright, and you are only financing the new one, then that that would be okay. But if you have a debt on the current property and the full price of the new property, then I don't recommend bridging finance.

Why invest in property?

Australians are among the most active property investors in the world, with an average of one in every three new mortgages arranged each month. Most of these investors are ordinary people with ordinary jobs earning ordinary incomes. So, why is property investment so popular?

Capital growth

Capital growth is the increase in value of property over time. The long term average growth rate for Australian residential property is about 9% a year. Importantly, because property markets move in cycles, property values go through periods of stagnation as well as decline. This is why taking an investment view of at least 10 years is important.

Note: if your investment property increases by 7.5% a year, over a 10 year period it will double in value.

Rental income

Rental income, also known as yield, is the rent an investment property generates. You can calculate this by dividing the annual rent by the price paid for the property and multiplying it by 100 to determine the percentage. As a general rule, more expensive properties generate lower yields than more moderately priced properties.

There is also usually a direct, inverse relationship between capital growth and rental income. Those properties producing a lower rental yield will often deliver greater capital growth over the long term.

Tax benefits

The Federal Government allows you to offset against your taxable income any losses you incur from owning an investment property.

For example, if the amount you receive in rent from tenants is $5,000 less than the cost of servicing the mortgage, and paying rates, water and other fees associated with the property, at the end of the year you can add that $5,000 to the amount of income on which you don't have to pay tax. If you work as an employee, with income tax automatically deducted from your pay, this means you'll receive a refund from the Australian Taxation Office (ATO) after the end of the financial year.

Low volatility

Property values generally fluctuate less than the stock market. Many investors say they experience greater peace of mind for this reason.

Leverage

Property enables far greater leverage than many other investments.

> ### Case Study
>
> If you have $100,000 in savings, you could invest it in a portfolio of shares, or use it to buy a property worth $500,000 by taking out a mortgage for $400,000. If shares go up by 10% during the year, your share portfolio would be worth $110,000 and you would have gained $10,000. If property goes up by 10% during that same year, your property would be worth $550,000 and you would have gained $50,000.

You don't need a big salary to invest. If you are buying to invest, lenders will take rental income, as well as your own income, into their assessment. If you already own your own home and have some equity in it, you may be able to use this as a deposit, meaning that you can buy an investment property without having to find any additional cash. If you don't own your own home and feel you may never be able to afford one, buying an investment property may be a good stepping stone to one day being able to afford your own home.

Investing In Property

Here are some tips to help you find the right rental property and reap the most rewards.

Unit or house?

House prices often increase in bigger strides than units, offering more potential for capital gain over time. But a rental home also comes with added responsibilities, including gardens and lawns (and sometimes a pool) to maintain. A unit or townhouse may not increase in value as quickly, but they are generally easier to maintain and may even be easier to rent for that very reason, depending on location, condition and size.

Location, location

Of course, you've heard this before. But location can mean different things when it comes to rental properties. Renters are often looking for maximum convenience, so consider properties near schools, major shopping centres and public transport. Spend plenty of time researching target areas, including recent property price movements and future predictions, rental vacancy rates and any proposed infrastructure improvements. You should also do some scouting as if you were a renter to get a first-hand look at the local market.

Remove the emotion

One of the worst mistakes you can make with any investment is to buy with your heart instead of your head. Remember, your rental property is not your 'home sweet home'. A well-presented property is desirable, but think sensible, not swank. Ideally, you want a neutral interior colour scheme, serviceable and resilient flooring and window coverings, a low-maintenance yard and good storage. And if buying an older style unit, look for one with an internal laundry, a garage or car space, and few stairs (unless there's a great view to be had higher up, which can add to the property value).

Don't forget the extras

An investment property requires regular financial commitment beyond the loan repayments. Make sure you have the capacity to cover land and water rates and any maintenance and repair costs. Tenants are entitled to repairs or replacements as quickly as possible under their rental agreement, so you will need to have the means to pay. Apartments or units also come with body corporate fees, which can run to thousands in some modern complexes with professional landscaping and shared amenities, such as swimming pools.

Cover your investment

Make sure you take out landlords' insurance. This will cover you for damage caused by a tenant and unpaid rent if a tenant skips out, in addition to other standard risks, such as a house fire or a storm. If you invest in a strata title property, make sure the body corporate has sufficient building insurance to cover the cost of rebuilding the complex at today's prices. It's often hard to work out what you need to cover versus what the body corporate covers. A good rule of thumb is everything from the wall paint inward is yours and everything outside of that is covered by the body corporate.

Any interest?

Many property investors take advantage of interest-only loans because interest payments are tax deductible. That means you're taking a punt that the property's value will increase over time, leaving you with a financial gain in the long run. This is a good strategy for high income earners who are taking advantage of negative gearing. If you choose to positive gear your investment (i.e. generate a profit from the rental income after costs), you might want to consider a principal and interest loan and use the profit to shave off the principal. Just remember, you will pay tax on any income from your investment. Talk to your accountant about your tax situation so your broker can find the right loan.

Taking ownership

Couples taking advantage of negative gearing should put the investment property mostly or fully in the name of the highest earner to reduce their taxable income. If you need both incomes to be considered in the lending equation, speak with your broker to get the right advice on the best ownership equation for your circumstances.

Appreciate depreciation

The ATO will give you a discount on your tax bill for wear and tear on property. It's known as depreciation, and can be a very handy windfall for investors, especially if you buy a new property. The formula is quite complex and depends on the age of your property, building materials and the various fittings. That's where a professional quantity surveyor comes in. For a fee (often around $600), they'll assess the property and complete a Tax Depreciation Schedule, which your accountant will incorporate in your tax return.

Manage your investment

Managing a property takes time and energy. If you don't have much of either to spare, you should get a professional property manager to advertise the rental, screen and select tenants, collect and pay the rent, co-ordinate repairs and maintenance, provide condition reports, and manage any disputes. Ask other local landlords for referrals to reputable managers. You should also conduct twice-yearly inspections yourself. Any associated costs, including travel and accommodation, are tax deductible. If you decide to self-manage, you will need to be well-versed on tenancy laws and prepared to organise repairs, including those that arise after hours. We understand every borrower has unique circumstances, and that some are more complex than others. We know from vast experience which lenders will work with investment customers who have more complicated requirements, and will negotiate on your behalf.

Commercial property and business investments

When it comes to investing in commercial property, you need to make sure you have the correct structure for the commercial purchase, and the entity has to be set up for asset protection. If you are buying a property for your own business, you want to make sure your personal assets are covered, and that you can't lose them if something goes wrong with the business. You also need to make sure that your structure for tax is right, and that comes back to your commercial interests.

> The structure is the most important thing when it comes to commercial lending. And the reason it is different is because we need to maximise your tax benefits for your asset protection.

So where do you get good advice?

You need to talk to a commercial property agent who actually knows their stuff because commercial properties are generally zoned for different usages. A commercial property could be zoned for industrial use, or it could be for office space. If you buy a property you intend to use for your business and you are a mortgage broker, if it is zoned industrial, you won't be able to have an office in that property. You need to make sure that the commercial agent gives you the right information so that you know the property is correctly zoned for the business.

When buying commercial property, your team of experts will also differ. You need a commercial mortgage broker who knows a little bit about accounting and tax, and a broker who can work with your accountant to make sure that the finance is structured correctly for acceptance by the bank. Your accountant may suggest a certain set up and a good broker will make sure that that structure is going to suit the bank.

For example, if your company has a trust set up and you want to buy that property through your trust, you need to make sure that the bank will actually finance the property through the trust. They might want it in a personal name or in a company name, not a trust.

So if you talk to a good commercial mortgage broker, she or he will know the ins and outs of the lenders and make sure that when the accountant sets up the company, it is in the correct entity.

Anyone can buy commercial property, and it is easier if you are not using it for your own business. If you are employed as a PAYG tax payer, earning a normal nine-to-five income, and buying a commercial property as an investment, that actually covers the income side of it. But if you are starting up a new business and don't have an income and you want to buy a business or a property, then you could fall into some difficulty because you are not earning anything. The bank is not going to lend you the money.

If you want to buy a commercial property, the deposit required is generally 30%. There is no mortgage insurance, which is a good thing, but you need a bigger deposit. If the property is a storage unit or something that may be hard to resell, then the bank will probably force you to have an even bigger deposit, because it is not something that they can easily sell if you default on your mortgage.

On a commercial lease, you pay to get the office set up the way you want it. If you then move out because your lease is up, you've got to put it back to the way it was. You might have to paint the walls, make sure the carpet is good, take out walls etc. if the owner wants it that way. The lease is a little different also because it's generally a five-year term with a five-year option. That means the tenant leases it for five years and then has an option to stay another five years. In a residential situation, it is generally a six- or twelve-month lease. There is no extra option. Basically, you may have to re-sign another lease and there is no obligation for the owner to renew your lease or give you that property for another 12 months. Plus, with a commercial lease, all the outgoings, such as strata fees, are covered by the tenant, not the owner of the property, so that is another good reason to buy commercial property.

However, commercial property is just not as sought after as residential property. If you buy a commercial property, you need to make sure that it can easily be resold if you want to sell it. It can be harder to sell a commercial property than a residential property. A commercial real estate agent might disagree with me, but that is my thought.

Commercial finance is very varied, so while one bank might not be willing to lend against a property in a particular suburb, another bank might be quite happy to do so. For instance, development properties are quite interesting to look at. At the moment, Westpac might have a good appetite for development finance, but Suncorp don't have an appetite for it at all. So it is a good idea to talk to a commercial broker to find out what sort of appetite the banks currently have for commercial business.

There is no such thing as a standard rate in commercial finance, so going to one bank will limit your options to the product and policy of that one bank and you may not get the best deal.

Commercial finance is done at 'rate for risk'. If you go to a bank that likes development finance, they might offer you an interest rate of 6%, whereas another bank that doesn't like it might offer you 8%. If you don't use a broker and you approach the bank on your own, you are not going to know that.

> ### ⊕ Key Point
>
> The big difference in commercial lending is that it is rate for risk, and all the banks will rate for risk differently. Commercial finance applies to anything commercial – buying a property, building a property, development – anything that is in the business space falls under these legalities.

Cash flow in business is a really big thing. You have to understand that the bank's advice may be biased. One bank might only lend you 65% against the type of security, so the approval will come for 65%. However, there may be other banks that will lend up to 80% against that same security, which means that your cash flow is not killed by having to put in 35% when you could have put in just 20%. The banks aren't going to tell you what the other banks are doing at the time.

The bank makes the final decision. You should consult a broker to get more control of your own situation and make sure you are getting the best deal. You can make a better decision by talking to a broker, because they can help you make an educated decision on which bank to use.

> Keeping business and personal interests separate is really important. If you've got personal security, try not to tie that up with your business. Try and keep it all totally separate if you can.

There are several different business structures you can have. It could be a propriety limited company, a trust, or even a property trust. They are generally the way to go. It is best to discuss this with your accountant, but a good finance broker is able to point you in the right direction. Most commercial properties will attract GST in the purchase price, but there is also GST included in commercial rent, so you want to make sure that your structure is going to give you the best tax advantage and asset protection for the business. That is really important.

Whichever structure you choose will totally depend on your current structure, your assets, your business, and that is probably more of an accountant's area of expertise. The bank generally prefers a propriety limited company or a trust, but this is something you should definitely discuss with an accountant.

Asset protection is more easily set up within a company, rather than in your personal name. If things are set up in your personal name and you do something wrong, it is easier to be sued and lose all your personal assets. You need to make sure your assets are protected, personally and in business.

When selecting your commercial investment team, you want to make sure they understand the complexities of commercial and business loans. Are they experts in commercial loans or do they mainly do residential? A lot of residential brokers say they do commercial, but they don't know much about them and that is really, really important. Talk to a commercial broker, not a residential broker that thinks that they know their stuff. I have a commercial broker in my own business because I don't think I know enough about the commercial side to write commercial loans.

Make sure you get the right lender as well. Ask them what type of businesses they finance? Do they have other requirements for the business? What kind of merchant facilities, bank guarantees, equipment finance is available?

Not all lenders will finance all types of businesses. To get help developing a long term strategy, work with a commercial broker who understands accounting and tax, and can work with you to grow with your business and cater to your business' funding requirements now and in the future.

You need a mortgage broker; you also need a really good accountant, a financial planner that you can work closely with to make sure that your strategy will work, and a commercial real estate agent. It is all about getting the right people. These professionals can give you ideas that you might never have thought of.

> ### Case Study
>
> Different banks will lend different amounts towards franchised businesses. Let's say you've got a Bright Eyes franchise. Westpac will give you 60%, but ANZ will only lend you 50% because Westpac might have too many Bright Eyes franchises and they don't want too many more. So they make it harder to get. That is why they limit the LVR (Loan to Value Ratio) that they are going to lend the client.

Key takeaways

To get ahead in business, and in general, you need to make some good investment decisions and you need to speak to the right people.

- $ Your mortgage broker will tell you what you can afford and which bank to use

- $ Your real estate agent will tell you about zonings and what you can do with the property

- $ Your accountant will tell you whether you are set up properly tax-wise, and whether the purchase is a good idea

- $ Your financial planner can do up a plan to make sure that your strategy is going to be suitable moving forward

It is about buying the right investment property, and having the buyer investment strategy that is going to suit you personally, not doing what someone else, your mate or your friend, tells you to do.

It is about getting good advice on your investments so that you get financial freedom in the long run.

Get the right experts and team members on your side, because if you select them well, they will help you get from point A to point B. Think about your future. And think about making your money work for you.

CHAPTER 4

Protecting your future and planning for the "what ifs"

Most of the strategies we have discussed are long term in nature, so we are talking about several years. We have a natural starting point and over time we build towards the outcome we desire. Insurance is there to protect us from the 'what ifs' — what if something happens and one of the key parties isn't able to get to that point?

In Australia, most people protect their car with insurance; they protect their contents and their home with insurance. But they generally don't protect the income-earning capacity of the person or persons who financed or bought those things. They don't protect their income, and quite often, when there is high exposure to debt, they don't protect the life or the financial interests of the people who are responsible for paying those things out.

⊙ **Key Point**

Insurance is a natural means of providing yourself with protection at a reasonably low cost. You are protecting the financial interests of the people that you are ultimately leaving behind.

Australia has a 'she'll be right' mentality. "Everything is going to be fine. I'm bulletproof. I'm going to work for the next 30 years and make money and nothing is going to go wrong." That is okay up to a point, like if you are single. I quite often hear people say, "Well, if I die, then so be it. It is not my problem anymore." But that changes when you have a partner and children and debt obligations that your kids have no capacity to repay. It is quite grown up to think about the topic of death when you are in your prime – your 20s, 30s, and 40s. You don't want to think that way, but unfortunately, it is one of those things that has to be considered. We, as mortgage brokers, try to raise the topic and make sure that is something you take seriously and you review along the way. Once the insurance is in place, it is far easier to say, "Okay, now she'll be right."

By taking out insurance, we look to protect the worst-case scenario, and the worst-case scenario, from a financial perspective, is the death of the breadwinner, or physical incapacity, or the inability to create an income by either of the breadwinners if you are part of a couple. We look to make sure that if one of those people is removed from the picture, the survivor or key parties aren't going to be left worse off financially. Obviously, if that person is the primary breadwinner and has a large home loan debt, the answer is generally yes, they are going to be worse off. We don't look to profit from death, but we need to mitigate against the financial impact of that person's removal.

Case Study

A single mother with a young son just moved into her new home with a mortgage and shortly after there was a very stressful incident, and she was unable to return to work for a period of time. She was handling a tragedy. She had only recently taken out income protection insurance when she took out the loan, and after a month of being incapable of work, the income protection kicked in. It continued for four months while she was going through all of her treatment. She said that without us she wouldn't have her home. That's pretty powerful. She said that the income protection insurance was the difference between keeping her home and losing it.

Case Study *(cont.)*

Another recent example happened to a husband and wife. They had a five-year plan to build their super and get to the point where they could retire. The husband was diagnosed with a terminal disease two years in, so he was not going to get to the point where he could retire. But because it was a terminal illness, we were able to claim on his death, even though he was not yet deceased. We have established everything now, so that even though it is inevitable that he is going to pass away this year, his wife is already set up and doesn't have to stress or panic from a financial perspective. It is all up and running and ready to go.

I had been meeting with this couple every year and as part of our discussions we would review his insurance needs. Because it was costing over a $1,000 a year, we would always ask, 'Do we still need this cover?' The response was always, 'Well, from a financial perspective, are we at the point where we could retire if something went wrong now?' and each year we said no. So we kept the cover and didn't cancel it, and again, that was the difference between the wife having a comfortable retirement and not. Obviously it is still going to be a stressful and horrible year, but her financial situation is catered to.

One of the things we get told quite frequently is, "I can't afford insurance premiums," and our response is usually to point out that if you can't afford the premiums now, how could you afford your debt repayments without a salary? Who pays the bills if you can't? For how long? How many sick days do you have currently with your employer? Ask yourself the question, does my employer love me enough to continue to employ me and pay me for three months after I physically can't work for them? And what about six months? And what about 12 months? Generally, most employers will look after you for a month, maybe two, but after that you are on your own.

And think about this: what becomes of the home when the breadwinner dies? That is another very important question. If the breadwinner is the person repaying the loan and they are removed from the picture and the mortgage is still there, what becomes of the home? Will the survivor have to sell the home to provide themselves with cash, or just to reduce or get rid of the debt obligation? Will they have to take the kids out of private school? Will they have to compromise?

It is one of those things that is always going to happen to someone else, and that's what people plan for. It will always happen to someone else, but everyone knows someone that it has happened to. You don't have to go too far to hear a story about someone who had to miss work for a long period of time because of an incident or a tragedy in their family. Unfortunately, it does happen.

As a community, we are living longer, and part of that is due to better health standards. We look after ourselves better, but we are also more susceptible to things like cancer, heart attack and strokes – things that 20 years ago were almost a death sentence or severely impacted a person's life. Now you can go back to work within a month after a heart attack, but if you've got income protection, you might be able to sit back and take an extra month or two to properly recuperate and take stock, then go back to work in a better state of mind.

Unfortunately, it does happen. For every 100 policy holders, we can assume there have been six or seven claims in the last two years, so statistically, it happens more often than people think.

There are four basic types of insurance

$ Death cover, which is the worst-case scenario, provides a lump sum benefit for the beneficiary or the estate in the event of death

$ Income protection, which protects the person's salary or income against an inability to work for a period of time, depending on the nature of the disability and how long the insurance will pay for things of that nature

$ Total, permanent disability, which is a pretty grim scenario, because it generally involves that person not being able to work again for the rest of their life. These are reasonably severe things – quadriplegia, diseases that attack the brain and mental capacity

$ Trauma or medical crisis – they are called both, but they are the same thing. These are generally significant health issues but things that people can bounce back from, such as heart attack, cancer, stroke. They are the big three and they account for about 80% of cases. You can have a heart attack, or you can fight cancer and have a good success rate and a good life expectancy beyond that, but the short term financial impact can be quite severe. It can be in the hundreds of thousands of dollars to attack cancer and even if you beat it, you are still $100,000 worse off

If I were to prioritise them, I would say income protection was the most important. If you talk to anyone about their financial circumstances for more than five minutes, you will generally talk about things that require income, things like repaying a loan, funding a retirement, raising or educating kids. All of that revolves around someone generating an income. We tend to take our salary for granted, but if we lost it, it would have a huge impact on our lives.

Death cover is pretty self-explanatory and the worst case scenario. If someone is diagnosed with a terminal illness and they are not likely to be around within 12 months, you can make a claim before they die, get the lump sum and start putting it to good use, whether that means reducing debt or putting money aside for children or partners.

With a total, permanent disablement, the benefit provides a lump sum that is designed to cover treatment or rehabilitation if they are going to need it on an ongoing basis.

For example, if someone is a quadriplegic or in a wheelchair, that person is very likely going to need to have their home adapted and renovated to accommodate that change to their lifestyle. Total permanent disability and income protection go hand-in-hand. In that situation, you have the rehabilitation costs and the medical cost as a lump sum, but you also have an ongoing need for income. When income protection kicks in, ideally it generates monthly income that covers living costs, whereas the total permanent disability lump sum benefit is there to cover those one-off costs.

> ### ⊕ Key Point
>
> Statistics say that a couple in their 30s have a greater than 50% chance that a medical crisis will befall one of them before they turn 65. That means that there is a greater than 50% chance that one party in any couple will have a need for a trauma insurance claim prior to their retirement, and that may be quite significant.

Most people in their 30s don't want to be thinking about big, nasty things like that, but that is the reality that we live with. We are living longer; we can survive cancer and we can survive heart attacks with greater frequency now, but the financial implications are still there.

You should also insure your assets, including the car, your home, the contents. It takes a lot of time and effort, and a lot of money, to save for and accumulate these things and without insurance, if something does go wrong, you've got to start again from scratch. Insurance is a small proportion of the total cost that would apply if you had to buy everything again, so if it is valuable enough for you to miss it, then you should look to insure it if you can.

Private health cover

We don't handle a lot of that, but private health cover can mean the difference between getting key medical assistance and being in a queue or having to compromise. It can also mean having to wait, or go into a room with five other people rather than having your own room and your own level of comfort.

Private health cover can assist with the financial impact of basic minor health events so that you don't have to think twice about giving yourself a base level of comfort from a health perspective. I always tell my retirees, "You can't put a price on your health." A lot of people don't want to spend money unnecessarily when they retire, so they'll forgo health related things. There is no point having lots of money but being sick all the time.

Protecting business interests

If you own your own business, there are a few different areas that you can protect with business insurance, and the first one is generally your business and the business' ability to generate income.

It used to be called Keyman Insurance, and essentially, if you've got one, two or three parties that are primary drivers of revenue for your business, you can insure them so that if they are physically unable to work for a period of time, the business income doesn't suffer. It is the equivalent of income protection, but for the business.

The second one, a very good, simple mechanism for business protection, is buy/sell agreements. If you've got multiple partners or business partners, they can cross-own business insurance policies so that if any of the business partners die or are totally and permanently disabled, the business can pay for premiums. In that event, the spouse of the respective person receives the benefit in the event of a claim, and the business value passes to the surviving business members. It is an unobtrusive and simple way of protecting the business without having to ask the spouse, assuming that the spouse is still alive, "How do we pay you out of your business interest?"

In one scenario, the spouse might come into the business and say that they will take over the deceased partner's role. For a variety of reasons that is generally not a great plan. The business owners that are actively running the business don't necessarily want someone lacking skills or experience to just come in and start trying to run it. So the partnership agreement and the cross-own business insurance can assist with reducing the impact of that, or removing that possibility.

Investment property insurance

There are a few insurances that go hand in hand with an investment property. Most importantly, you will need building insurance, and then landlords' insurance, which most people have.

On top of this, we recommend all the normal insurances that fall under financial planning, which are life, TPD, trauma.

Lender's Mortgage Insurance?

Lender's mortgage insurance (LMI) only covers the bank. If you don't have a 20% deposit, the bank will charge mortgage insurance, a one-off fee that can be added to your loan if you don't have enough equity in your property.

If the bank needs to foreclose on your loan because you haven't made payments or something is going pear-shaped, then LMI covers the bank, not you. You have to pay quite a large sum for LMI, and if something does happen, it is the bank that gets the money. You never get your money back if you default; it only covers that bank, not the client.

Rather than paying for LMI, a better solution might be to take out death cover for the same level of cover. If you repay the loan down from $500,000 to $250,000, and you've still got that $500,000 death cover, if that person passes away, the loan is repaid, and the survivor, or the estate, is still left with $250,000.

LMI is only there to protect the bank's interest. They will get paid, but there will be no surplus that goes to the estate or anyone else. The lender is very much protected in that regard and that is why they love the LMI policy. They capitalise it on to the loan so people don't notice the financial impact as much, but it potentially adds time to the term of the loan, and it is only protecting the worst-case scenario for the bank.

If the bank is forced to claim against LMI, you do get the home or the property, but that is all you get. I'm not saying it is a terrible cover, but it is definitely more in the lender's favour. They know they are going to be repaid regardless of what happens, so they move on happily. But as an individual, and if that is your only insurance, you are still susceptible to all those things discussed before — heart attack, cancer, stroke, death, income protection events.

Insurance in a superannuation policy

Most people don't really want to give this topic serious thought because it is too daunting. If we ask them about insurance, they answer, "My super handles it."

A lot of insurance policies are held within superannuation funds or within superannuation, and there used to be a cliché in the industry that group policies held within super were cheap and nasty. They are no longer cheap. Now they are just nasty, because there have been a number of claims, specifically in the last five years, and the premiums have gone up quite considerably on these policies. So they are no longer any cheaper than what we call retail policies or individual policies.

Most super policies are group cover, so they are negotiated between the insurer and either the employer or the industry body. If they are looking to reduce premium costs, they will take away benefits or dilute the efficiency of the policy by taking away certain benefits, and that is totally beyond the control of the individual. So the fund member, who owns the policy, has no power. If the fund decides to take out benefits for cancer, for example, the fund member has no power to say, "Hang on, I've got a family history of cancer and I want that protected." With retail cover, you deal directly with the insurer; you have a full assessment and then come to an agreement, and that policy cannot be changed unless both you and the insurer agree on it. So you hold the power.

> We have seen significant changes to group cover in the last five years. Premiums are significantly higher and benefits have been reduced, and in some cases just taken away without the insured person even being made aware of it, or having any power to influence it.

We are very much advocates for having insurance cover through super, but now you can actually negotiate retail policies, so you have an insurer and an insured agreement, and it can still be paid by the super policy, but it is not one of those group covers where the individual has no power.

Estate planning

A will essentially states the individual's wishes as to how their estate is distributed in the event of their death.

A solid will addresses the wishes of the deceased and makes sure it prioritises the people that are most risk, or stand to be the most at risk, in the event of their death – so usually children and spouses.

If you pass away without a will, the money usually still goes to the right place, but it may take longer, and often allows far more possibility of being contested. Family and money are two flash points for stress or heated discussions. Having a will in place and setting it up so that the money goes to the right parties at the right time is key. But once you've got it, you have peace of mind, knowing that if something happens today, your wishes are going to be carried out.

Wills are quite an adult topic. Children, teenagers, and people in their early 20s, who don't have beneficiaries and, at that stage, don't have much in the way of assets, don't really need a will. We always stress that you should consider a will, but generally it is more relevant in the husband/wife or partner situation, even de facto, but definitely when there are children involved, or parties that would stand to be worse off in the event of that person's death. Everyone should consider a will, but you definitely need one when there are people involved who stand to be worse off if you were to pass away.

Will kits were very popular about ten years ago, and they are still around. They are inexpensive and relatively straightforward. The issue we have with them is that, generally, you cannot make specific requests – you can't say I want this asset, or this investment to pass to this person. They are quite simplified. Also, they can be contested.

There are a lot of lawyers that can easily poke holes in the wording of a will kit will and the enforceability of certain wills. Phrases change over time and some will kits from the past may no longer be correctly worded, which may make them unenforceable now. We always suggest that you speak to an estate planning professional. They can point out things that you might not ordinarily think about off the top of your head, as in scenarios where you want specific assets to go to certain people, or about what might happen from a custodial point of view.

It is not as expensive as people think. You can get a pair of wills drawn up for a husband and wife for well under $1,000 and, as we said, it's something that, once you've got, hopefully gives you peace of mind. You do need to review them every few years to make sure that they are still current and still reflect your wishes, but generally they are easy to review.

Estate planning encompasses the will, but also a lot more. It includes things like power of attorney. There is the standard power of attorney, which essentially gives someone the capacity to act on your behalf, and there is also an enduring power of attorney, which covers the situation where you lose mental capacity. A standard power of attorney generally expires or is not valid from that point, whereas an enduring power of attorney can continue even if the individual's mental capacity is lost.

Estate planning also covers death benefit nominations within superannuation, which is very important. We just talked about superannuation being a life insurance policy, but it has its own set of estate rules or eligibilities. There are other considerations, including custody of children in the event of death, and the timings of bequests of certain estate assets for children, who may be too young to have the financial literacy to handle it themselves.

◎ Key Point

Wills and estate planning are daunting, adult topics, but if you have beneficiaries that stand to be at risk in the event of your death, handle it once and get it done correctly, even if it costs some money. You can then continue on, knowing that you have the peace of mind that it is under control. The risk is that if you don't address it and something goes wrong, it is your beneficiaries and family members that suffer.

Mistakes to avoid with insurance

You must shop around. There are well over 25 insurers in Australia that can issue life insurance products, and different insurers target different markets at different times in different demographics. Insurance risk levels are based around the risk of a particular occupation. White collar workers who work behind a desk have a different risk level to someone who works in the mines on heavy equipment.

Different insurers target different demographics and occupational categories, so it is handy to know which insurers are more aggressive or better value in those areas. And they all have different small print within their contracts. Some insurers will issue a contract that won't cover a blue collar worker for a period greater than five years, and other providers will. It is very important to get the best outcome or the insurance provider most likely to give you the best outcome.

Insurers also review their costs periodically, not every year, but they review their cost of insurance and their premium rates. In the last few years, a lot of insurers have reviewed their costs and, unfortunately, they very rarely review them down. So insurance premiums, even for existing policy holders, have gone up over the last few years.

While it is great to get the right cover and have the right policy on day one, you still need to review it. It might no longer be the best value two years or five years down the track. It's the same with your mortgage and anything with varying numbers.

⊕ Key Point

The best time to take out an insurance cover or policy is when you have no need for one. It is when you are in your 20s or 30s and you don't have the beer gut, you don't have the stress levels of 20 years of work, you don't have all the other things that happen to men and women in their mid to late 40s. It is when you are ideally fitter and healthier and the insurers are willing to take you on as a client.

If you take out cover at that point, there are options for level premiums, which means the premiums won't rise as you get older. If you approach the same insurer at 45 as opposed to 25, the 25-year-old is going to get a significantly lower premium, but also, their premium won't rise as significantly over time.

A common mistake is insuring the wrong thing. We can over-insure and under-insure. If we have four different types of cover, that means that we aim to cover all possible scenarios. But if we insure to the fullest extent in every circumstance, it can cost a lot of money. We try to work out a portfolio of insurances that will cover all of the worst case scenarios from a financial perspective within the client's cash flow and servicing abilities. And we try to place the ownership of the premiums or the policies so that they have the most beneficial impact from a tax perspective. Certain premiums are tax deductible, and we can also have your superannuation potentially pay for some premiums.

You must give insurance the proper consideration. Don't fall into the trap of thinking that you have it covered because it is in your super. It may be in your super, and your employer may have the cover, but it is still in your best interests to consider these things and make sure that you have the appropriate cover; even if it is in your super, it should be appropriate and the right level and the right type of cover. It is a serious topic and it is something that requires a little more attention.

The biggest mistake you can make is taking insurance for granted and not shopping around.

Using a professional is the equivalent of using a mortgage broker. It gives you access to someone who has the experience and knowledge of the various providers, and knows who can source the best coverage for the best value and the best premium price. Every insurance contract is different; every insurance offering is different, so knowing which insurer has the best definitions for certain issues and conditions that may be applicable is valuable information.

For example, if your family has a history of cancer, knowing which insurer has the best definition for those sorts of things will mean you get the appropriate protection.

The role of an insurance broker is to be the liaison between you and the insurance provider, so we do quite a bit of lobbying with insurance underwriters and assessors to try and get the best possible outcome in terms of the occupational risk rating, which dictates the premium. With medical issues, we know how to provide enough information so that we can legitimately avoid, where possible, exclusions or decline responses.

Key Point

Probably most importantly, an insurance broker is there to assist with insurance claims. We don't take insurance for the lowest premium or the pretty prospectus, we take it because we don't want the financial implications of having a claim event. In the event that you do need to file a claim, the broker is there to help and make that as stress-free and as painless as possible.

To work out whether you have the right insurances, you need to be asking these questions:

$ Who pays the bills if I can't?

$ What would become of my home if the breadwinner passed away?

$ What would we do about the kids' education if our income was removed or halved? Who would repay the debt? Can we stay in our own home?

$ What if we have more kids?

$ What if we have a change in marital status?

$ What if I change jobs? You might have an exceptional policy for your previous job, but what if you change career paths and the existing cover is no longer the best in the market?

> We review our insurance policies for our clients every two years as a minimum, we suggest every year. It doesn't necessarily mean that we change anything; we just review it in the market to make sure it still represents good value and it is still appropriate and doing what you want it to do.

From the opposite perspective, you should also consider financial windfalls. An easy example is winning lotto. It's rare, but if you win lotto you might be in a position where you don't need insurance anymore because you have repaid the debt and now have a significant savings amount. Inheritance is a similar situation. So over time, as you work, you reduce your debt, and increase your super and savings. You raise the kids and ultimately the kids move out of home, so the need for insurance naturally should diminish over time. There is an end point, but we always say that the need for insurance doesn't expire until you no longer need the insurance, and that is what our review discussions aim to ascertain.

Talk to your broker about their insurance - what their speciality is, what their credentials are, whether they are a Certified Financial Planner, whether they are members of the industry body, the financial planning association. How do they get paid? Are they paid via commission? Are they paid by fee for service? Who are they aligned with? Are they owned by or influenced by their licensee? For example, if they are aligned with one of the major banks, then they are probably going to promote that major bank's insurance products, whether they are the best in the market or not. Also, do they get extra commissions or extra loadings or incentives to recommend a certain provider over other providers, because that may influence their decision making as well.

That is how we suggest you approach someone initially, and obviously, you should ask them if there is a fee involved for the initial advice. If you are shopping around and want to speak to two or three different advisers, you might end up paying two or three lots of fees for one lot of advice.

As part of their role, a financial planner should be an insurance person as well. Not everyone is; some planners are specialists in certain fields,

Smart Money

and that is something else you should ask. If you are addressing your insurance needs, a financial planner should have the capacity to address your other needs as well.

In our business as mortgage brokers, we also talk about your superannuation and your cash flow management, budgeting and other strategic things. If you just want to address your insurance, then an insurance broker is good for that, but that person might not necessarily be thinking of the other implications of their advice. They might not be thinking about the effect the premiums might have on your super balance or other estate planning issues.

Superannuation

Most people's thoughts on superannuation goes like this – "I can't touch it until I'm 65 years of age, so I don't care about it now. I'll just let it be. It is mandatory that a certain amount of my wage goes there, but I just get the statement once a year, I look at the numbers, and then I file it."

Our argument is that you should get your super headed in the right direction as soon as you possibly can. The biggest asset with investments is time, giving your investments time to run through market cycles and generate growth over longer periods. People in their 30s and 40s have the time, prior to standard retirement age, to get their super moving. It is just that sometimes they don't have the inclination.

⊕ Key Point

We always say review it; make sure it is invested in a way that you are comfortable with. We call it the 'sleep at night' factor. We don't want people lying awake at night, looking at the ceiling, wondering if the market is doing nasty things. It has got to be an investment portfolio that you are comfortable with, but once you know that, you can afford to selectively ignore it, knowing that at least it is doing the right thing for you, and it is growing over time.

The worst thing I see, and it still happens, is someone who is in their 60s or within a year or two of their retirement, and they come to see me and say, "Right, here is my superannuation," and it is generally the first time they have given it a serious look in many, many years. They have missed out on a lot of opportunities just because they didn't look at it until it was too late.

The benefits of compounding returns and time are very much underrated and overlooked by younger people because it is not something they put a lot of thought into.

When you get your first job, say you are earning the minimum wage, superannuation is mandatory. But most people at that age sign up to the superannuation fund that their employer suggests. There is not a lot of thought put into it, and over time, there is not a lot of money put into it. At that level, basic funds do the job. The super payments need to go somewhere, and as long as it is going to a legally compliant superannuation fund, that is fine.

But at a certain age, and it is different for everyone, usually around the mid-20s, people start to develop at least a certain amount of financial literacy. That is when they should be looking at these sorts of things. Now, that doesn't mean they need a fund with all the bells and whistles, but that is when they need to make sure that their money is moving in the right direction and that it is invested in a way that they are comfortable with.

A lot of funds are what we call basic retail funds or industry funds or employer-sponsored funds, and you get what you pay for. They are low cost, but there are not a lot of intricacies or options within them. A lot of those funds have four or five or six investment options and you just pick one and put the money in that. They don't have a lot of other features or things that you can add on, and if they do have insurance available, it is usually quite limited.

Once you have accrued a certain dollar figure, and again it is different for everyone, but usually around $50,000-$60,000, you really should take it a little more seriously than just getting the statement and putting it to one side. You should look at opportunities to invest with funds that have greater diversification, more investment options, more bells and whistles, more things that you can do with your funds to take greater ownership of them.

The natural progression beyond that is your self-managed super fund (SMSF), and that tends to be for people who have specific desires that can't be met by your standard superannuation offering. They want direct property in their fund; they want direct shares in their fund; they want to potentially borrow money to leverage their superannuation and grow it at a more significant rate; or they just have very specific investments or assets that they want to have in their fund that your normal retail offering doesn't provide.

Key Point

There are tax benefits for superannuation and insurance. Super is a very good cash flow management and tax management tool. The government has put limits on our annual ability to put money into superannuation, but it does provide fairly generous tax concessions within those limits.

An accountant or a tax professional can suggest levels of contributions and their tax implications. The next logical step is to speak to a financial planner about the two phases of superannuation – there is the accumulation phase while you are growing it and accumulating, and then there is the pension phase when you start drawing from it, and again, there are tax implications on both ends.

You should never start a plan without knowing where the logical end point is, or what the final implications are. Speaking to a financial planner and/or a tax advisor will help you identify the benefits going in, but also ultimately what is going to happen at the end when you retire.

If you close one super fund to go to another fund, know what you are losing. In certain circumstances, if you have an insurance policy within that fund, that policy would be cancelled upon roll-over, so you would lose the cover and you may not get it again. Also, know the fee implications if you are moving from one fund to another, or entering a new fund. Ask if there is an exit fee, so that if in a year's time you decide this is not the fund for you, you are not going to get hit with a big fee on exit.

Know what you are signing. Superannuation is a 20-, 30-, 40-year investment. If you are going to be stuck in a dud fund for 40 years, unfortunately "I didn't know" is not the best excuse. Just know what you are signing before you go into it, and know the worst-case scenario. If you speak to a planner, they will guide you in the right direction so you don't make a bad decision that you are stuck with for what could be decades.

One important thing to realise is that if you've got five super funds because you have changed jobs five times, or you've just set up a bunch of different super funds, you could be paying duplicate fees. It is not the end of the world, but if you are paying administration costs of $100 once that is bad enough. If you are paying that five times a year, it does eat into your retirement savings. It is a saving that you could have; sometimes you are saving by not spending.

Investments

In any investment strategy, your biggest assets are time and the ability to leave those strategies to perform.

Also, in broad terms, basic diversification is important. The old clichés are clichés for a reason – don't put your eggs in one basket. Know that markets run in cycles, and that comes back to your time frame. You don't want to sell an asset at the wrong time because you are forced to. If you've got the time and you believe in the asset, give it the time to grow and go through its natural cycle.

Your financial planner will prepare a statement of advice. It's what we used to call a financial plan. Engage a planner who has the capacity to address your needs. If you have an insurance broker and that is all they do, they will not be in a position to consider your cash flow, superannuation, and things of that nature. Go to a planner who has the capacity to address all the issues, and as the consumer and client, you have the power. Keep looking until you find the right one.

A good financial plan will cover all eventualities. At a core level, we would cover super, insurance, cash flow; we would consider tax situations where relevant, and then estate planning, because they are, to an extent, intertwined. If you consider all those things, you can put the perfect plan in place, but you still do need to review it. The one constant that we have is changes – in government, changes to rules, the tax office changes the rates, the markets change over time, be it property or shares or interest rates. As individuals, our own situations can also change. As we get closer to retirement, our needs are different; if we are raising a family, we have different needs to someone who has just started a job and doesn't have any dependents.

⊕ Key Point

With investments, always consider the worst-case scenario and mitigate against it. We have already touched on life insurance, but think about what if would happen if interest rates were to go up by two or three percent. What if you didn't have a tenant for a long period of time and you didn't have that income? If you ask yourself those questions and your response is not a worst case for you, but is something you can cope with, then you can continue with a little more confidence.

We have clients whose ages range from the early 20s to the mid-80s, and they are still actively seeking advice and reviews from us. You become an adult, technically, at the age of 18, but you really become an adult at a different time, when you realise, "Geez, I have kids, I have these super statements that I never look at, I have all these different things that are quite adult, daunting things to think about, but I don't want to address them." That is generally when a financial advisor can assist, because you let them do it for you, as Homer Simpson says.

Chapter 4

> ◉ **Key Point**
>
> A lot of people reach a point where they know they need a will, but they put it off till next year. They know they should take more care or interest in their super, but they put it off till next year. If you've got kids, or you've got debt, you should really consider your insurance. Don't put it off till next year. That is really when you should sit down, make it as painless as possible for yourself, and speak to someone and let them assist you. Handle it all in one dealing, one appointment or one series of meetings, and then you can move forward with peace of mind, knowing that all of those situations are covered from a financial perspective, regardless of what happens.

There are hundreds and thousands of planners out there offering different things. Your standard statement of advice fee can be anywhere from $800 to $8,000. It depends on what you want addressed, the complexity of your needs and how in depth you want the advisor to go. In terms of value, somewhere in the realm of $1,000 to $4,000 should cover everything that you are trying to do, within reason.

An insurance-only situation, where you are just addressing your insurance needs, is generally cost-free, but the advisor will receive a commission. The commission is paid by the insurer, not you, but if the advice you receive is purely insurance advice, it will be reasonably limited. It will hopefully cover that specific area with some complexity, but it is not going to cover your super, cash flow and other things. In terms of value, if you get great advice on day one, that's terrific. The value flows over the years that follow, an extra couple of percent in terms of returns, be they investment or super, and hundreds of thousands of dollars over decades.

Minimising tax legally can add value, and it's often overlooked. People look to reduce their tax but they miss out on fairly simple strategies that can give them a tax benefit year on year. There are also other things for older people, including Centrelink assistance, maximising your aged pension, minimising your tax in retirement, prolonging the longevity of your investment portfolio, catering to estate planning so that you have

Chapter 4

that peace of mind, knowing that in your eventual death, the money that you have accumulated goes to the appropriate parties.

My advice for couples is to talk to each other about what you want to do, what your priorities are. All too frequently a couple will sit with me, and one of them will start talking about what 'we' want, and then the other person looks at them and says, "Hang on, that's not what we want at all; that's what you want." Talk about exactly what you want as individuals, but also as a couple, because your spouse's priorities might surprise each of you.

> The cliché that I always use is you can't start too early with your financial planning, but you can start too late. You might be at a reasonably simplistic stage, where you are repaying debt and your needs might be a little bit simpler. But if you start planning early, a small benefit adds up incrementally over time, and the compounding effect can add tens of thousands and hundreds of thousands of dollars to your end point.

We always suggest that you set up a plan, but you don't just sit on your hands. Put the plan in place and then review it, monitor it, visit your plan again and adapt. If you need to adjust it, adjust it. The best plan today is not necessarily going to be the best course of action in five or ten years. And again, the sooner you start the better.

Don't let yourself be daunted by a million different options. Someone in their 20s could do any one of hundreds of legitimate investment strategies, but the sheer number of them scares them off and so they do none of those. So at least talk, research, and find some things that you like and are interested in and investigate them. Talk to professionals, and once you have honed in on a couple of things that you have an interest in and might benefit you, investigate those further. You might identify some things that you are very happy with and you choose to establish.

Finally, don't be fooled by the flashing lights and the fountains. There are a lot of financial planners and professionals that talk the good game and have the fountain out the front and a good sales pitch, but ask them if they invest in what they recommend. Ask them what the worst-case scenario is. Ask them how much experience they have, and make sure that you're comfortable with the person you are going to be dealing with potentially for 10, 20, 30 years. I call it the 'mum and dad' rule — would you send your mum and dad to them and know that they are going to look after them?

Retirement planning

Very, very basic retirement planning starts the day you open your superfund, because that is going to be a key component. People in their teens and 20s don't think that way, but that is the basics of it. Retirement planning is generally the culmination of planning that you have hopefully done throughout your working life.

Pre-retirement planning starts a minimum of five to seven years prior to your planned retirement, and ideally longer than that. But there are things to do in your 50s — as you repay debt and turn your focus to building your superannuation, make sure that your estate planning is airtight. Look to minimise your tax on an ongoing basis, enhance your returns, build your super, and get it to a point where the day you walk away from your job, your super is in a position where you can start utilising it to generate income or provide you with income on a sustainable basis.

Transition to retirement is a very good strategy, but governments do change the rules periodically, so that's a good strategy right now. Making superannuation contributions is a good strategy. Investing money into super for the future is a good, long term strategy. After that, it is just about all those generic investment strategies — getting the money in the right place, and giving it time.

$ Centrelink assistance — if you are eligible for it, you should aim to get Centrelink Assistance

$ Minimise your tax legally — in retirement you should aim to either pay minimal tax, or in an ideal world, no tax

The need for growth doesn't end at retirement, but the need for equity is instantly greater at retirement because you no longer have a salary to replace any short term investment losses. Then it is just about monitoring and managing your investments and keeping abreast of all the rules, legislations and opportunities.

⊕ Key Point

We are living longer and the government is making it harder to qualify for the age pension, and it is only going to get harder still. In 20 years, the aged pension has gone from being an expected component of everyone's retirement income to becoming a supplementary piece. Now, by the time people in their 30s and 40s retire, it is only going to be a safety net. It is only going to be there for people who haven't built an investment base that is sufficient to generate their own income.

In my experience, the longevity argument is, strangely enough, the opposite of the insurance argument. When I talk to people about their life insurance, my clients say, "She'll be right," but when I talk to them about their retirement planning and the potential to be retired in 30 or 40 years, they say, "No, no, no, I'll be dead in ten years." Pessimism about mortality is misguided. People think that they are going to be retired and they won't make it to 70 or 75, but statistics show that, at the moment, people are living into the mid-80s, and it is only going up.

💡 You have to factor in that you are going to have to work for longer, or you are going to have to compromise later in life, from a financial perspective.

Key takeaways

The sooner you start, the better you'll be in the long run. Go for value, not necessarily cost. Obviously, we want low cost, but we also want the best possible value and sometimes the cheapest isn't the best.

Chapter 4

Research your planner as much as you research anything else. Whichever investment professional you deal with, have some confidence that they can do what they are going to commit to, and that they are going to do something that meets your priorities.

Don't be daunted by short term results. Any investment with any sort of volatility is going to go up and down over time. If you believe in your course of action and you are comfortable with the investments or assets that you are investing in, then stick with it, give it time. But again, make sure you review it, because there might come a time when a change is warranted. Just know that, and give your core strategy time to do what it needs to do.

CHAPTER 5

Putting it all together

The main thing you need to do is talk to a professional first up; get all your information from a professional person and do not talk to your family and friends about your finances.

You want to make your mortgage work for you, so making sure that you are in a product that's suitable for you at the time is very important, as is revisiting it. Talk to a financial planner about getting the right investments in place so that, moving forward, you are going to secure your financial future.

If you are a first home buyer, familiarise yourself with what happens during the mortgage process and also after the mortgage process. It is helpful to keep a schedule so that you know what happens and when.

We have discussed the mistakes to avoid, and what you should and shouldn't do throughout life around managing your finances. We looked at the pros and cons of credit scoring and the things that the banks look for that might help you get a better score and a better chance of getting your loan approved. Then we went through getting into an investment, what is possible and what is out there for you, making sure you are covered by insurance, and we also discussed your superannuation and how to make sure that all your investments are going to set you up for the future.

◉ Key Point

The biggest piece of motivation I can offer is to keep your finances top of mind and don't let your investment just sit and stay there forever. You need to keep visiting it, and don't be slack with it. Be educated instead of uneducated. Utilise a professional to help make the decisions. Don't get them to make the decisions for you, but make sure you are actually making an educated decision when it comes to your finances, not just a guess, because that is when you could do the wrong thing.

If you have read this far, you are at a crossroads now. You can continue doing what you have been doing, which is likely to be uninformed, and just accept what is happening. Or there is option B, which is what we have been talking about in this book. The sooner you get your finances in place, the wealthier you are going to be. If you want to be wealthy in the future, you need to start working towards it now. You also have to realise that it is not just about a mortgage; it's about ensuring that everything you can do is being done.

Now that you know the process is going to be easy, you might be more willing to get started. Falling into financial stress at a young age, like I did with my credit card, sometimes makes you aware of what could happen later on, so sometimes that is a good thing.

One of our little clichés is 'get rich quick', but most people get wealthy slowly. Start early and give yourself time and know your options. Learn from those who have been through it. They've tried it and they've honed it and that is generally where professionals can help. Hopefully they've seen most situations and know the tips and traps and can keep you on the path.

People think it is all too hard, and it's not. They think they don't need to know because it doesn't affect them until later. But if you give it to a professional to look after, they will make it easier. It is our job to hold your hand or take you under our wing and make the whole process easier. And you don't have to pay us anything. The bank pays us.

If you don't think it is worth it, you are going to have a very sad retirement with no money. If you wait for something magic to happen, prepare yourself for disappointment. You have got to do something to get something. It's the same as any sport — you need to practice. You need to get started to do things — a couple of dollars a week to start really adds up over time. It works for kids, but it works for adults, too, so don't wait until the last minute and just hope that the magic will happen.

Key Point

What I would like you to do after reading this book is take a bit more interest in your financial future and realise that it is just as important as your health, because they go hand in hand. Once you do that, the next logical thing would be to actually get motivated and go and speak to someone about it.

Think about what you want, what you want to achieve. Most financial planners offer a free initial consultation and if you go and speak to them, they can advise you on a course of action that is going to work for you. The worst-case scenario is that you don't speak to anyone at all. You wait ten years and then you find out about something you wish you had done ten years ago.

Sometimes it is riskier to do nothing than to invest in something, or buy a property, or look at this, or look at that. Some people are so risk adverse that they do nothing, but they don't realise it is riskier to do nothing.

What's the next step?

Want to get smarter with your money and mortgage?

Most people struggle to manage their money properly. Even with regular salaries coming in, they spend too much and end up further and further in debt - and the money worries and stress always follows.

Most people don't know how to correctly setup and manage their mortgage. All too often we hear that "a loan is just a loan, they are all the same", which is false. All loans are not equal and if you don't know what to do you could be set up the wrong way, you could be paying too much, and you could be restricting your options for the future.

But it doesn't have to be that way. You don't have to struggle with your money and you don't have to navigate the minefield of mortgages alone.

It's also important that you get expert advice from a professional who understands the finance and mortgage market inside and out. It's simply too difficult and there's too much to try and do it all yourself.

You should speak with a FinanceCorp mortgage professional today, and get an expert on your side - to ensure you're set up correctly, not paying too much, and are thinking about your financial future.

And the best part is, I will do everything for you!

Start a conversation with me today - I will help you get smarter with your money, mortgage and financial future.

☎ Call me on: **0417 395 949** OR

✉ Send an email to: **traceym@financecorp.com.au**

Tracey Franco
DIRECTOR / MENTOR

ABOUT FINANCECORP

We are FinanceCorp

Our motto at FinanceCorp is *Finance Made Easy*!

We live and breathe this for each and every one of our clients. Our role as a mortgage broker is so simple and we never lose sight of this. We are here to match the right home loan to each of our clients. This must suit their needs both now and in the future. We don't play favourites with lenders because we are solely focused on finding the right loan for you.

An important part of this process is ensuring things are kept simple and stress-free for our clients. Our team of professional brokers will ensure that you are kept informed at every stage and feel happy and confident. We are absolutely committed to providing our clients with a service that will exceed their expectations.

15 Years on...

All of the Finance Managers at FinanceCorp are fully qualified, trained and experienced mortgage professionals who live and breathe finance. They joined our team because they share the same vision as our company.

Every one of our Finance Managers is motivated by getting the best results for their clients, every time. All of our staff operates under the industry code of conduct.

Our Sole Focus Is On You!

Why choose FinanceCorp?

$ There is no charge for the FinanceCorp service. We don't have favourite lenders; we simply help our clients choose the right loan from the right lender, based on what our client's need and/or want is

$ We offer a choice of over 25 top lenders — that's hundreds of products! Your FinanceCorp Finance Manager can help you compare the loan products of over 25 different lenders quickly and easily

$ We understand your needs. We understand that everyone needs to know how much they can borrow. It is a very important question. Not only can we tell you this very quickly, we also give you specific loan details and tell you how much your repayments will be just as fast. We will also tell you all fees involved with your purchase / refinance etc

$ We help our clients choose the right loan. Your FinanceCorp Finance Manager will inform you about the loans that are right for you. We will discuss the details of each loan that suits you best

What happens when I contact you?

Step 1: phone call

This first contact is a quick and simple 5-10 minute chat on the phone. Your broker will ask you a few questions to establish your requirements and gain an understanding of your personal situation to find out how we can help.

Step 2: calculate

Sit back and relax - at this stage, we do all the work. Our role as your broker is to sift through the hundreds of options to find the home loan that will best suit your personal circumstances. We will work hard to find the right loan.

Step 3: meeting

We offer a flexible service. This means that you can meet at our office, or we can come to you at a time and place that is more convenient. We offer appointments that may be outside of business hours, as well as on the weekend.

Our customers

It sounds so impersonal to call our clients customers, as our Finance Managers work so closely with every client that they soon develop a strong relationship with them.

This means that many of our clients feel they can trust their personal Finance Manager to look after their needs.

We work very hard to gain and continue to keep this trust. We believe that this will build long term relationships rather than a one-off sale.

Our mission statement

It is our vision to be the best Financial Service provider in Australia. To deliver a superior service, in a friendly and courteous manner to our valued customers, with our main aim being their financial well-being. We will emphasize building strong long term customer and lender relationships to achieve a high level of customer satisfaction.

Our values

Here at FinanceCorp, our values are based on "Doing The Right Thing" through:

$ Honesty and Integrity

$ Mutual Respect

$ Quality

$ Trust

$ Teamwork

Our support goes to

FinanceCorp is proud to support many local businesses and charities.

SECOND HARVEST

Second Harvest offers low cost food centres throughout the Perth Metro area to support low income families, as well as offering employment opportunities.

INTENSIVE CREW

FinanceCorp is also proud to support the Intensive Crew, the WA division of the Intensive Care Foundation.

Contact Me:

Office Address: Unit 1, 18 Blackly Row
Cockburn Central WA 6164

Phone Number: 0417 395 949

Email: traceym@financecorp.com.au

Website: www.financecorp.com.au

GET YOURSELF ON TRACK WITH THE FINANCECORP APP

Do you like to keep track of your finances and where your money is going, or do you need to get yourself into a financial routine and start budgeting?

Then the FinanceCorp app is for you, as it will help you track and organise your personal finances on a daily basis. It is powerful and easy to use while at home, or even if you are on the go.

The FinanceCorp Mortgage Calculator App is an app made simple for on-the-go calculations. This app will assist to give you quick estimates of what your assessable income tax may be, estimate your savings amount for a deposit and how long it will take you to get there, plus much more…

Our app contains a number of calculators such as:

$ Income Tax Calculator

$ Property Stamp Duty Calculator

$ Savings Calculator

$ Repayment Calculator

$ Target Wealth Calculator, and more

Valuable Resource

Download our FREE App from our website at:
www.financecorp.com.au/downloads

10 REASONS WHY YOU NEED A MORTGAGE BROKER

In this age of technology, where an endless amount of information is available at our fingertips, it is easy to think we can do all the research and investigation that it takes when buying our next property.

However, the reality is quite different, unless you have weeks of spare time and energy, as well as the capacity to store and sort through the hundreds of home loans on the market, and consider other variables such as fees and conditions.

Here are 10 REASONS why a mortgage broker will prove to be invaluable:

1. **It makes financial sense.** In most instances, your mortgage broker's service is free. This is because lenders pay mortgage brokers a fee when they connect them to borrowers

2. **Mortgage brokers work for you, not the lender.** We all know that banks and other lending institutions are keen to sign you up to their products. Their real interest lies in making as much money as possible from the interest that you will pay over the life of the loan. Alternatively, a mortgage broker will put your financial needs first and find the loan that will best match your circumstances

3. **Spoilt for choice.** You can rely on a mortgage broker to give you plenty of options. They have access to hundreds of different loans from a host of lenders, in fact far more than you will encounter if you choose to go it alone. You will find that mortgage brokers have access to some of the more boutique and wholesale lenders who typically don't advertise to the mum-and-dad property buyers. These lenders often have fantastic products and are also eager to gain your business

4. **Spare the legwork.** By enlisting the services of a mortgage broker, you can let them do the leg work when it comes to the loan application process. This will not only make life easier for you, but it can give you a better chance of gaining quick approval. This is because a mortgage broker knows what individual lenders require and makes sure your application is correct before submitting it

5. **Service when it suits you.** One of the great benefits of using a mortgage broker is that they can come to you at a time that is convenient for you

6. **Perfect match.** It is a common misconception that banks don't like mortgage brokers. The truth is, banks generally like mortgage brokers as they typically put forward applicants who are going to meet their criteria. This can be good news, particularly for higher-risk borrowers as it can avoid them being rejected and having a red flag on their credit history

7. **Avoid the pitfalls.** It is typical for lenders to use terms that entice borrowers to choose their products. These can be things such as honeymoon offers, exit fees and fixed rates. All of these can seem confusing to the average home buyer. Your mortgage broker will carefully consider your specific circumstances and work through all the various lenders' products. They will assess specifics, including establishment and long term fees, as well as terms and conditions to ensure you are not paying more than you should over the life of your loan

8. Borrowing within your means. When you use a mortgage broker to obtain your home loan, you are less likely to be over-stretched and find yourself in financial difficulty later. Some lenders may allow you to borrow to capacity, or even offer a loan that may not be quite right for your situation. A mortgage broker will always recommend the loan that makes the most financial sense to you

9. Switching is simple. There are times when you may want to change your loan. This may be due to refinancing, buying or selling the property, or a change in circumstances. Your mortgage broker can undertake all of the investigation and paperwork for you. It is not unusual for your mortgage broker to liaise with your conveyancer to keep things moving so that settlement occurs on time

10. Get a health check on your current home loan. The home loan market can change frequently with the move in interest rates. At any time, you can ask your mortgage broker to simply take a look at your home loan, your personal circumstances and the home loan market and give you an update. This may simply be recommending that you stay with your current loan or that you move lenders or change products. Whatever the outcome is, you can feel relaxed knowing that you have been given a recommendation based on current information

COMMON QUESTIONS

For home buyers

How much money can I borrow?

Everyone's situation is different and it is all of these unique circumstances that will indicate your own borrowing capacity. If you want to get an understanding of how much you can borrow and what your repayments are likely to be, you can use the calculator tools found on our website – www.financecorp.com.au. These calculators are designed as a guide only.

If you would like to determine precisely how much you can borrow and what your repayments will be, you need to speak with your FinanceCorp Finance Manager.

How do I choose the loan that's right for me?

Your Finance Manager has access to hundreds of different home loan products across a huge variety of lenders. We can provide you with a guide to the different loan types and features which will help you understand the different options available.

But importantly, it is your Finance Manager that will do all of the work for you. They are the experts when it comes to knowing and understanding the different types of home loans available to you. They will make a recommendation about which product will best suit your individual needs.

How much do I need for a deposit?

Your deposit is normally paid when you sign a Contract of Sale. Usually between 5% — 10% of the value of a property, which you pay when signing a Contract of Sale (called an Offer of Acceptance in WA).

As a rule, all banks require a min 5% of the purchase price as a deposit. However, there is one exception - Keystart only requires a 2% deposit. Keystart has strict lending guidelines which you will need to follow. Speak with us to discuss your options for a deposit. You may be able to borrow against the equity in your existing home or an investment property.

How much will regular repayments be?

Again, there are tools available on our website that can be used as a guide when calculating your home loan repayments. As well as there being a huge variety of home loan products, there is also an assortment of different options available when it comes to loan repayments. Your Finance Manager can talk these through with you.

How often do I make home loan repayments — weekly, fortnightly or monthly?

You will find that most lenders offer flexible repayment options to suit your individual needs, such as your pay cycle.

If you aim for weekly or fortnightly repayments, instead of monthly, you will make more repayments in a year, which will reduce your principal loan and shorten the life of your loan.

However, if you choose interest only repayments on your new home loan, then your repayments will have to be monthly and this will not reduce your loan.

What fees/costs should I budget for?

There are a number of fees involved when buying a property. To avoid any surprises, the list below sets out all of the usual costs:

$ Stamp Duty — this is the big one. All other costs are relatively small by comparison. Stamp duty rates vary between state and territory governments and also depend on the value of the property you buy. You may also have to pay stamp duty on the mortgage itself

$ To find out your total Stamp Duty charge, visit our Stamp Duty Calculator on our website: www.financecorp.com.au

$ Legal/conveyancing fees — generally around $1,000 – $1500, these fees cover all the legal rigour around your property purchase, including title searches

$ Building inspection — this should be carried out by a qualified expert, such as a structural engineer, before you purchase the property. Your Contract of Sale should be subject to the building inspection, so if there are any structural problems you have the option to withdraw from the purchase without any significant financial penalties. A building inspection and report can cost up to $1,000, depending on the size of the property. Your conveyancer will usually arrange this inspection, and you will usually pay for it as part of their total invoice at settlement (in addition to the conveyancing fees)

$ Pest inspection — also to be carried out before purchase to ensure the property is free of problems, such as white ants. Your Contract of Sale should be subject to the pest inspection, so if any unwanted crawlies are found you may have the option to withdraw from the purchase without any significant financial penalties. Allow up to $500 depending on the size of the property. Your real estate agent or conveyancer may arrange this inspection, and you will usually pay for it as part of their total invoice at settlement (in addition to the conveyancing fees)

$ Lender costs — Most lenders charge establishment fees to help cover the costs of their own valuation as well as administration fees. We will let you know what your lender charges but allow about $600 to $800

$ Moving costs — don't forget to factor in the cost of a removalist if you plan on using one

$ Mortgage Insurance costs — if you borrow more than 80% of the purchase price of the property, you'll also need to pay Lender Mortgage Insurance. You may also choose to take out Mortgage Protection Insurance. If you buy a strata title, regular strata fees are payable

$ Ongoing costs — you will need to include council and water rates along with regular loan repayments. It is also important to take out building insurance and contents insurance. Your lender will probably require a minimum sum insured for the building to cover the loan, but make sure you actually take out enough building insurance to cover what it would cost if you had to rebuild. Likewise, make sure you have enough contents cover should you need to replace everything if the worst happens

What is the First Home Owner Grant and can I get one?

This is a grant available to Australian citizens or permanent residents who wish to buy or build their first home, which will be their principal place of residence within 12 months of settlement. Contact us directly to find out how much grant money you could receive.

For those thinking of refinancing

Can I get a mortgage where I pay less than I'm paying now?

With lenders adjusting their rates outside of the Reserve Bank, now is a great time to shop around or check that you have the right loan for your needs.

We're a great starting point. It will depend what interest rate you're currently paying, what type of home loan you have (e.g. fixed, variable, interest only, line of credit) and what features you want in your loan. We can quickly explain your options.

Can I consolidate credit card or other debts into a home loan?

This is one of the reasons many people refinance. The advantage is that you pay a much lower interest rate on a mortgage than for most other forms of debt — e.g. credit cards, overdraft facilities, personal loans. Providing you have sufficient equity in your property, you may be able to consolidate all your debt in a home loan. If you take this option though, it is important to make sure you maintain your repayments at their current level or you could end up paying more over a longer period. Speak with us today to discuss your personal needs.

How does refinancing work?

Your mortgage broker will work through the refinancing process in much the same way as they did when you originally took out your home loan. The refinancing process will consider a variety of home loans that best suit your current or changing needs. You will be given a few options with your new home loan and your broker will work closely with you to help you determine which one is right for you.

Why refinance?

The reasons that people refinance are as personal and unique as their situation, but there are some general reasons that people choose to refinance. These may be one or more than one of the following:

$ **Pay off debts:** many people have accumulated additional debt outside of their home loan, including personal loans, car loans and credit card debt. The repayments on these can become quite a burden, and typically the interest being paid is very high. Refinancing can allow you to eliminate other debt and create only one repayment instead of juggling multiple payments

$ **Renovations or home improvements:** you need additional funds to renovate, extend or make improvements to your home. Typically, any improvements you make to your home will add value. By using the equity in your home, you can tap in to this rather than funding it yourself

119

$ **Purchasing another property:** if you have some equity built up in your home, you can use this equity to purchase another property. Property is not the only option when considering how to leverage your equity. You can also look at shares and other investment options

$ **Using your savings:** some people have money sitting in a typical bank account earning low or minimal interest. If this is you, you could consider putting this money in an offset account, where your money will reduce the interest payable on your mortgage

$ **Changing interest rates:** interest rates are reviewed monthly by the Reserve Bank of Australia. This means that over time there can be a considerable amount of movement (either up or down) and you could be taking advantage of this

$ **Needing flexibility:** if you are currently in a position where you are overstretched with your mortgage repayments and are concerned that you may default in the future, this is the right time to consider refinancing. We can often help you before you get into trouble

$ **Changing the type of mortgage you have:** over time your needs will change and you may wish to re-examine the type of mortgage that you have. You may want to switch the type of mortgage you have, for example, moving from a fixed rate to a variable rate of interest or vice versa

When is a good time to refinance?

The answer to this question is really simple – whenever it makes financial sense to do so!

In the past, people took out a mortgage and typically stuck with the same product and bank until it was paid off some 20 or 30 years later. Nowadays, there are a lot more options available to you. It makes good sense to revisit your mortgage every 2-3 years. Your mortgage broker can run a quick health check on your home loan.

This will determine if you are getting the best deal given current interest rates, or whether there is a product on the market better suited to your needs.

What fees/costs are involved in switching mortgages?

Penalty fees could apply if you're paying off your current mortgage early, especially if you're exiting a fixed home loan. But these may be offset by repayment savings when you switch home loans. We'll walk you through any fees that will apply in your circumstances.

How much money can I borrow?

We're all unique when it comes to our finances and borrowing needs. Get an estimate on how much you could borrow with our clever loan options tool. Chat to us when you're ready, we can help with calculations based on your circumstances.

What is Lender's Mortgage Insurance (LMI)?

LMI is an insurance policy that your lender may require you to take out to insure them against the possibility of you defaulting on your loan.

Why would I be required to take out LMI?

There can be many reasons for your lender requiring you to take out LMI. Each lender has particular policies that it must adhere to. Factors that get taken into consideration are: the type of loan, the amount of deposit compared to how much you wish to borrow, the value of your property, and other factors such as perceived risk of default.

For example, if you are borrowing more than 80% of the property value, you will be required to take out the insurance policy on behalf of your lender, which your lender will organise.

The cost of the premium varies according to the amount that you are borrowing. The more you are borrowing, the higher the premium cost.

Who pays for it?

The lender takes out the policy on your behalf. The full premium amount including the GST on the policy is your cost. Like any insurance premium, once it has been paid it is non- refundable.

How often do I need to pay for this?

It is a one-off premium, upon settlement of the loan. In some circumstances the premium can be added on to your mortgage.

How does it work?

The LMI policy, like most insurance, is only drawn upon if something happens. In the case of LMI, the policy comes in to effect if you default on your loan. After a default, the bank may not recover enough from the left over proceeds after the sale of your property default. The LMI policy allows them to make a claim on the policy for the outstanding amount.

Does this policy cover me too?

No, it does not. It covers the lender against the risk of you not meeting your repayments when they fall due. Even if you default by not making repayments, you are still required to repay the whole loan amount to your lender. It is often confused with Mortgage Protection Insurance, which covers you for loan repayments in the event of an unexpected situation occurring, for example unemployment, disablement, or death. Other insurances which may also benefit you in providing you peace of mind are: income protection, trauma, and permanent disability. Don't forget that you will be required to take out building insurance and it is strongly recommended to insure your contents as well.

If this policy does not cover me, then how does it benefit me?

It may mean that the bank will not agree to provide you with the loan to purchase your intended property. It may also mean that you may have to wait till you have saved the right amount of deposit – 20% in most cases

— which may cause a delay in you owning a property, possibly for quite some time. Sometimes the benefit of paying the LMI will outweigh waiting, especially as it may be easily offset by the capital growth in property that may occur over that same amount of time.

Still confused?

Remember if there is anything that is not clear or that you still find confusing you should speak to your Mortgage Broker. They are here to help you and make you feel comfortable at every stage of the process.

⊙ Valuable Resource

Have you got another unanswered question on your mind? We are happy to take questions anytime, just email or call us:

Email: admin@financecorp.com.au

Phone: (08) 9417 5550

EXPLAINING THE LOAN PROCESS

It costs nothing to get in touch. We can quickly help find out how much you can borrow and which loan may suit your needs, plus answer any questions about the process. Find out what's involved in taking out a loan, from start to finish.

How does the process work?

Arrange a pre-approved loan

If you haven't started your property search, or are still looking, a pre-approved loan can be useful. It gives you a clear picture of what you're spending limits are and gives you peace of mind that if you find a property you really interested in, you can move quickly to make an offer. And it may put you in a stronger negotiating position than other potential buyers who don't have pre-approval.

Find your property

Make sure you do plenty of homework when you're on the hunt for a new property. Research property prices in the area, potential capital growth and existing and planned infrastructure, such as roads, public transport, schools and shops. If you're unfamiliar with property values in the area, consider a full valuation carried out by a registered valuer before making a final decision.

Make an offer and sign a Contract of Sale

Whether you buy property at auction or make an offer on a listing, your agreement with the vendor only becomes a legal commitment when a Contract of Sale (Offer of Acceptance in WA) has been signed by both parties. This contract will confirm the selling price as well as any terms and conditions. Your commitment will usually be subject to lender approval, a building inspection report and a pest inspection.

The period from signing a Contract of Sale to Settlement – when the property becomes legally yours – is usually six weeks (shorter in some states, such as Queensland).

Note: even if you have a pre-approved loan, your lender will still need to complete a valuation of the property you have chosen before issuing full approval.

Pay a deposit

A deposit is required once a Contract of Sale has been signed by both parties (sometimes called 'exchanging contracts'). You won't yet have access to your home loan, so your deposit will need to come from savings or elsewhere. You may also be able to arrange a deposit bond until settlement.

Appoint a conveyancer

You will need a solicitor or conveyancer to check the legalities of the Contract of Sale. Your conveyancer will also check all rates and taxes have been paid, check land use or building approvals for the property and order any relevant searches. They may also help sort out any inspections.

On settlement day, the conveyancer will check the correct amount of money has been transferred from your lender to the seller, and all fees – such as Stamp Duty – are paid, so you can take legal ownership of the property.

Cooling off period

If you didn't buy your property at auction, you may have a cooling off period during which you can cancel the contract, although there may be a small penalty. Cooling off periods vary from state to state so check with your relevant state authority to find out what your rights may be.

FINDING THE RIGHT HOME LOAN

There are literally hundreds of home loans available, with new products emerging all the time.

As a broker we can help you find a loan that suits your particular needs, help you complete the paperwork, professionally package it with your supporting documents and submit it to your chosen lender. Here's a snapshot of the main types of home loans and some of their pros and cons.

Variable rate loan

Standard variable loans are the most popular home loan in Australia. Interest rates go up or down over the life off the loan depending on the official rate set by the Reserve Bank of Australia and funding costs. Your regular repayments pay off both the interest and some of the principal. You can also choose a basic variable loan, which offers a discounted interest rate but has fewer loan features, such as a redraw facility and repayment flexibility.

Pros

$ If interest rates fall, the size of your minimum repayments will too

$ Standard variable loans allow you to make extra repayments. Even small extra payments can cut the length and cost of your mortgage

$ Basic variable loans often don't come with a redraw facility, removing the temptation to spend money you've already paid off your loan

Cons

$ If interest rates rise, the size of your repayments will too

$ Increased loan repayments due to rate rises could impact your household budget, so make sure you take potential interest rate hikes into account when working out how much money to borrow

$ You need to be disciplined around the redraw facility on a standard variable loan. If you dip into it too often, it will take much longer and cost more to pay off your loan

$ If you have a basic variable loan, you won't be able to pay it off quicker or get access to redraw if you ever need it

Fixed rate loan

The interest rate is fixed for a certain period, usually the first one to five years of the loan. This means your regular repayments stay the same regardless of changes in interest rates. At the end of the fixed period you can decide whether to fix the rate again, at whatever rate lenders are offering, or move to a variable loan.

Pros

$ Your regular repayments are unaffected by increases in interest rates

$ You can manage your budget better during the fixed period, knowing exactly how much is needed to repay your home loan

Cons

$ If interest rates go down, you don't benefit from the decrease. Your regular repayments stay the same

$ You can end up paying more than someone with a variable loan if rates remain higher under your agreed fixed rate

$ There is very limited opportunity for additional repayments during the fixed rate period

$ You may be penalised financially if you exit the loan before the end of the fixed rate period

Split rate loans

Your loan amount is split, so one part is variable, and the other is fixed. You decide on the proportion of variable and fixed. You enjoy some of the flexibility of a variable loan along with the certainty of a fixed rate loan.

Pros

$ Your regular repayments will vary less when interest rates change, making it easier to budget

$ If interest rates fall, your regular repayments on the variable portion will too

$ You can repay the variable part of the loan quicker if you wish

Cons

$ If interest rates rise, your regular repayments on the variable portion will too

$ Only limited additional repayments of the fixed rate portion are allowed

$ You will be penalised financially if you exit the fixed portion of the loan early

Interest only

You repay only the interest on the amount borrowed, usually for the first one to five years of the loan, although some lenders offer longer terms.

Because you're not also paying off the principal, your monthly repayments are lower. At the end of the interest-only period, you begin to pay off both interest and principal. These loans are especially popular with investors who plan to pay off the principal when the property is sold, having achieved capital growth.

Pros

- $ Lower regular repayments during the interest only period
- $ If it is not a fixed rate loan, you have the flexibility to pay off, and often redraw, the principal at your convenience

Cons

- $ At the end of the interest only period you have the same level of debt as when you started
- $ If you're not able to extend your interest-only period, you could face the possibility of increased repayments
- $ You could face a sudden increase in regular repayments at the end of the interest-only period

Line of credit

You can pay into and withdraw from your home loan every month, so long as you keep up the regular required repayments. Many people choose to have their salary paid into their line of credit account. This type of loan is good for people who want to maximise their income to pay off their mortgage quickly and/or who want maximum flexibility in their access to funds.

Pros

- $ You can use your income to help reduce interest charges and pay off your mortgage quicker
- $ Provides great flexibility for you to access available funds
- $ Consolidate spending and debt management in a single account

Cons

$ Without proper monitoring and discipline, you won't pay off the principal and will continue to carry or increase your level of debt

$ Line of credit loans usually carry slightly higher interest rates

Introductory or honeymoon

Originally designed for first-home buyers, but now available more widely, introductory loans offer a discounted interest rate for the first 6 to 12 months, before the rate reverts to the usual variable interest rate.

Pros

$ Lower regular repayments for an initial 'honeymoon' period

Cons

$ Loans may have restrictions, such as no redraw facilities, for the entire length of the loan

$ You may be locked into a period of higher interest rates at the expiry of the honeymoon period

Low doc

Popular with self-employed people, these loans require less documentation or proof of income than most, but often carry higher interest rates or require a larger deposit because of the perceived higher lender risk.

In most cases, you will be financially better off getting together full documentation for another type of loan. But if this isn't possible, a low doc loan may be your best opportunity to borrow money.

Pros

$ Lower requirement for evidence of income. May overlook non-existent or poor credit rating

<u>Cons</u>

$ You will probably pay higher interest than with other home loan types, or may need a larger deposit, or both

YOUR GUIDE TO COMMON LOAN FEATURES AND BENEFITS

Interest only repayments

You only pay the interest on the loan, not the principal, usually for the first one to five years although some lenders offer longer terms. Many lenders give borrowers the option of a further interest-only period. Because you're not paying off the principal, your monthly repayments are lower. These loans are especially popular with investors who pay off the principal when the property is sold, having achieved capital growth.

Extra repayments

If you pay more than the required regular repayment, the extra amount is deducted from the principal. This not only reduces the amount you owe but lowers the amount of interest you repay. Making extra repayments regularly, even small ones, is the best way to pay off your home loan quicker and save on interest charges.

Weekly or fortnightly repayments

Instead of a regular monthly repayment, you pay off your home loan weekly or fortnightly. This can suit people who are paid on a weekly or fortnightly basis, and will save you money because you end up making more payments in a year, cutting the life of the loan.

Redraw facility

This allows you to access any extra repayments you have made. Knowing you have access to funds can provide peace of mind. Be aware lenders may charge a redraw fee and have a minimum redraw amount.

Repayment holiday

You can take a complete break from repayments, or make reduced repayments, for an agreed period of time. This can be useful for travel, maternity leave or a career change.

Offset account

This is a savings account linked to your home loan. Any money paid into the savings account is deducted from the balance of your home loan before interest is calculated. The more money you save, the lower your regular home loan repayments. You can access your savings in the usual way, by EFTPOS and ATMs. This is a great way to reduce your loan interest, as well as eliminate the tax bill on your savings. Lenders provide partial as well as 100% offset accounts. Be aware the account may have higher monthly fees or require a minimum balance.

Direct debit

Your lender automatically draws repayments from a chosen bank account. Apart from ensuring there is enough cash in the account, you don't have to worry about making repayments.

All in one home loan

This combines a home loan with a cheque, savings and credit card account. You can have your salary paid into it directly. By keeping cash in the account for as long as possible each month you can reduce the principal and interest charges. Used with discipline, the all-in-one feature offers both flexibility and interest savings. Interest rates charged to these loans can be higher.

Professional package

Home loans over a certain value are offered at a discounted rate, combined with discounted fees on other banking services. These can be attractively priced, but if you don't use the banking services you may be better off with a basic variable loan.

Portable loans

If you sell your current property and buy somewhere else, you can take your home loan with you. This can save time and set-up fees, but you may incur other charges.

CHECKLIST OF DOCUMENTS FOR APPLYING FOR FINANCE

Most lenders require the same documents to approve a loan. Make sure you bring the documents below to your meeting with your broker to help fast-track your loan application.

This is a general checklist so some of the documents may not apply to you. Your broker will confirm which documents you need.

Personal identification

$ 100 points of ID are required. A current Passport or Birth Certificate = 70 points. Drivers Licence = 40 points. (Please note if these documents are in your maiden name, you will also need to provide a copy of your Marriage Certificate)

$ Other documents that help build up 100 points include: a Medicare card, Credit card, ATM/Debit card, Council Rates Notice, Pensioner Concession card, Health Care card, Tertiary Student ID card

Income details

$ The two most recent payslips from your employer. (Ideally these will show the company name, number of payslip and year-to-date income figure)

$ The most recent Group Certificate (now called a Payment Summary) from your employer

<u>If self-employed:</u>

$ The last two years' personal and business tax returns and ATO assessments

$ Other income details

<u>You may also need:</u>

$ Rental income statements or bank accounts showing rental income for any investment properties

$ Proof of share dividends or interest earned

$ Centrelink letter confirming family tax benefits

$ Centrelink letter confirming permanent government pensions

$ Private pension group certificate or statement

$ Proof of any other regular, ongoing income

Additional documents for refinancing

$ Documentation on your existing loan including the date the loan commenced, loan period and any financial penalty payable if you exit the loan early

$ Statements for the last six months for any existing home loans and personal loans

$ The most recent Council Rates Notice and building insurance policy on the property or properties being offered as security

Credit cards

$ If you have credit card debt, statements for the last six months

$ If you don't owe anything on your credit card, the most recent statement

Additional documents if you already own a home

$ Statements for the last six months for any existing home loans or personal loans

$ Your most recent credit card statement

$ Copy of the Contract of Sale for the property you're buying

$ Statements for the last six months to show your savings/investment history. (This could include share certificates, savings account statements, term deposit statements, etc)

$ If other funds are being used for the purchase, evidence showing where the funds are held

$ If other funds are being given to you, which are not already in your bank account, you will need a Statutory Declaration from the person giving you the money

Additional documents for First Home Buyers

$ Statement for your First Home Saver Account, if you have one

$ Statements for the last six months to show your savings/investment history. This could include share certificates, term deposit statements, etc

$ If other funds are being used for the purchase, evidence showing where the funds are held

$ If other funds are being given to you, which are not already in your bank account, you will need a Statutory Declaration from the person giving you the money

$ Your most recent credit card statement

$ Copy of the Contract of Sale for the property being purchased

Additional documents for investors

If you already have investment property:

$ Evidence of income such as rental statements

$ A copy of the tenancy lease

$ A Council Rates Notice

For the investment property you are purchasing:

$ Copy of the Contract of Sale for the property being purchased

$ A letter from a property manager indicating likely rent for the new property

Additional documents for borrowers seeking a construction loan

$ A copy of a valid builder's fixed price tender, including all specifications

$ A copy of Council approved plans

NO DEPOSIT HOME LOANS

There are options available to home buyers who do not have a deposit to purchase their own home. One such option is a guarantor home loan.

Guarantor home loans

A guarantor home loan is a type of mortgage where the parties who are purchasing the property gain assistance from a friend, relative or family member. The person acting as the guarantor will use the equity in their own property as security.

Guarantor loans tend to be very popular with first home buyers. Many young people who are looking to purchase their own home often struggle to save the necessary deposit required by many lending institutions, or may simply be unable to get a loan by themselves. There can be a range of other scenarios in which someone may not be able to get a loan and these can often give rise to using a guarantor mortgage.

Before you take out a guarantor home loan there are a few important things you should consider.

Advantages

$ **You will not need to pay mortgage insurance:** Your lender will view your mortgage differently if you have another security property. They will consider it to be low risk and this means you will not need mortgage insurance. Mortgage insurance can be expensive and not having to take it out can save you thousands of dollars

$ **You do not need a deposit:** If your guarantor has enough equity in their property, you will not need to pay a deposit on your home. This will allow you to borrow 100% of the purchase price on your property

$ **The guarantor can be removed down the track:** Taking out a guarantor home loan is not forever. You still have the flexibility to remove the guarantor from the mortgage once you have enough equity in your home

Disadvantages

$ **The guarantor carries liability:** The guarantor on your home loan is liable for part of your debt. This means that if you default or miss a payment, the person acting as guarantor must meet these commitments. This liability is limited to the amount of security given by the guarantor, usually this is 20% of the purchase price

$ **Limitations when buying and selling:** There are some restrictions around selling the security properties. You need to fully understand these limitations prior to going guarantor

Other options: Smart Families

If you cannot find someone who wants to act as guarantor, there is now a new product on the market that may be a viable alternative. In some cases, the person who is considering acting as your guarantor may not wish to put their own property at risk.

The Smart Family Home Loan is an arrangement where your parents lend you the money you need; it is a formal arrangement that is managed by your lender. There is no guarantor relationship that exists. A Smart Family Loan allows you to borrow up to 20% of the purchase price of your property from your parents. It is considered to be a formal loan and interest is charged at half the interest rate on your mortgage. Having access to these funds will mean that your parent's home is not used as security (as per a Guarantor Loan) and you will not require mortgage insurance. Further, you will still be able to access other programs such as the First Home Owners Grant and the stamp duty concession.

The bonus in this arrangement is that your parents will receive ongoing monthly repayments and will also have access to a share of the growth in the land value on the property. Flexibility is built in, whereby the loan from your parents may be written off at any time as a gift. You may be able to buy them out of their share of equity in the property, and in the event of a sale, whether forced or not, your parents receive their share back. They also have no obligation to take over repayments that are not being met, or put their own home at risk.

Still need more information?

Guarantor Home Loans are a very attractive option but it is important that all parties involved fully understand the process. We are here to help guide you through this process. We can meet with you and your guarantors together or individually.

The world of Finance Broking is very complicated and crossing t's and dotting I's is so important. I was very fortunate to have Tracey Franco mentor me when I began my journey as there was so much to learn and she helped keep my stress levels low. Because I was able to learn and be mentored by Tracey, I now have a good understanding of how to write a loan for the best results and keep up with the ever-changing rules and regulations. Tracey is always there to answer any questions or concerns and her level of support is second to none. Tracey has a wealth of knowledge and is top of the game.

Susan Briggs, Finance Manager

As a newbie to business, I was unsure of many things. Tracey helped with my confidence in many areas. Such as how to present our business to others, how to extend our networking circle and how to show appreciation to clients and associates. Tracey has been a fantastic mentor and a model to look up to. I am very grateful to have her guidance and insightful feedback. I value her advise and friendship dearly.

Lucy De Abreu, TDA Building Inspections

Tracey operates a couple of successful businesses. She is very knowledgeable and giving of her time and know how. She is extremely helpful and enjoys seeing other businesses succeed.

I met Tracey during the COVID lockdown and she invited me to join a group where she was mentoring other businesses. She was extremely knowledgeable and giving of her time and business experience. She helped connect me to other businesses going through a similar journey.

Tracey is very positive and business minded. She is always active in her business and always willing to give advice and help when needed. She has operated several businesses in her time and is always looking at ways she can help people. I love her can-do attitude which is very inspiring.

Rae Bateman, Elevate Business Solutions

www.ingramcontent.com/pod-product-compliance
Lightning Source LLC
Chambersburg PA
CBHW071702210326
41597CB00017B/2293